PVT Mills Gabriel
ACO, 3rd Pl
1st BN, 34th
165th IN BDE

2000 Dixie RD
Ft Jackson, SC 29207

MW01235467

INTO HIS PRESENCE

Now and Forever

by

Linda Warner

Illustrations

by

Andrew Cobb

One of my most excellent English students.
From the graduating class of 2011.
A young man of many talents and exemplary character.

Xulon
PRESS

Praise for the Book

I know God can use us in mighty ways when we give Him our heart. 2 Chronicles 16:9 tells us the following: The eyes of the LORD run to and fro throughout the whole earth, to show Himself strong in the behalf of them whose heart is perfect toward him. There is no doubt that Linda has positioned herself with an open heart and a willing spirit to be used as a vessel to communicate the power of God's love. Her message is needed now more than ever. People today need the Love of Christ more than ever. His transformative power and resurrective ability is what's missing at the core of every non-believers life. Linda's new book, *Into His Presence*, will help bridge that gap. Her message of hope, healing, and regeneration will share the faithfulness of God's promises with non-believers and will serve to refocus and restrengthen even the most ardent believers.

Dr. Dan Yachter
CEO of Yachter Family Chiropractic Center, World's largest
God-centered Wellness Clinic
Author of the book: Doctor of the Future
International wellness speaker and consultant

*

While scripture needs nothing added to it and certainly nothing taken away, sometimes the emotional infusion of life experiences can breathe new relevance into a verse read a hundred times. Linda Warner touches the heart with her eloquent stories in 'Into His Presence.' Fresh and insightful, she captivates your attention and connects with your heart by shining a light on the truths of God's word.

Eric Reinhold, Author of the Annals of Aeliana
Ryann Waters and the King's Sword
Ryann Watters and the Shield of Faith
www.ryannwatters.com

*

"In the Beginning" shows how God created the universe. Although this is a fictional story, nothing contradicts with what the Bible says. Instead, "In the Beginning" presents a creative vision of how God did it. If anything, this helps me to see how creative God is and how wonderful and mighty His power is. The description of creation makes me stand in awe of His good work.

An unsolicited comment about the creation story –
Erik Steenekamp, tenth grade honors English student at
Orangewood Christian School.

*

Linda Warner's stories have a way of cutting through to the soul of human existence and reaching you where you live. They are universal, yet somehow you feel as if each one was written specifically for you. Her grasp of literary style, her heart, talent and God given inspiration weave together to unravel the complexities of the human condition and lead you directly to the warm safe arms of the loving Father who longs to protect and adore you. Are you longing to know peace; with yourself and with life? Are you lonely or hurting, or feeling an emptiness gnawing at the innermost core of your being? Is something missing in your life, or the life of someone close to you? Then enter into the world contained herein, and with God's grace a light will shine to fill the darkness. You will smile, you will weep and you will ponder how complexity can also be simplicity. You will be entertained and you will be changed (as I was!). Who knew unlocking the secret to life and eternity could be so much fun! These stories were an integral part of the transformation of my life, and the peace and joy that surpasses all understanding being mine. I pray God's blessings on all who read this book, and on its author for submitting to His will.

Gregory B Holm, Ph.D.

Dedication

In my imagination, there has at times appeared a vision too lovely for human expression.

I picture myself sitting upon a fragrant, Galilean hillside with Lissie, Sue, Noell, Terry, Laurie, Lisa, and Marilyn, all of us reclined at His feet, awestruck by the wonder of His words, the love in His eyes, and the power of His presence.

With these dear ones, I have enjoyed countless, precious moments contemplating His endless love and amazing grace. With them, I have come to know and enjoy the Savior ever so much more intimately.

To Elise Armfield, Sue Murton, Noell Grier, Terry Munz, Laurie Carneiro, Lisa Laustsen, and Marilyn Amundson, I dedicate this effort. In eternity, may we walk hand-in-hand into His presence. Glorious thought!

*

I proclaim my unconditional love and gratefulness to God for the five men around whom my life revolves: husband Paul, sons Daniel and Timothy, and grandsons Aiden and Peyton, along with my two precious daughters-in-law—Joan and Joy.

I give special thanks to my son Timothy whose encourage-ment made this book happen.

*

To all who have suffered, may these words bring encouragement.

So What's It All About?

Entering into His presence!

The greatest gift I have ever received is the apprehension of just one profound truth—that life everlasting and joy unending is available at no cost to us, for King Jesus paid it all.

It is the unspeakable privilege of eternally abiding with the Creator and King of the Universe. Like the thief on the cross, we only need to ask. When He enters our lives as Lord, we become "new creatures."

Then what?

The realities of this planet's Fall do not evaporate like dew. But clearly, how we live through each sorrow, each fear, each disappointment reveals a mysteriously-radical change. Like Peter, we must affirm truth: "Lord, where else would we go?"

I have, I must admit, contemplated the sorrow shrouding this planet and have longed to retreat to a lush, lonely island where I could live out my life in tranquility. Then I heard Pastor Michael Yussef's words: "We are here to be warriors for Christ. Do not flee the battle," he said in essence. Yes, this life is often pervaded with exhausting distress. All around us are hard hearts and rebellious spirits and the walking wounded.

So, how do we enter into His presence and persevere as warriors for His kingdom?

Not always but often it seems, SUFFERING becomes the pathway leading to the highest awareness of God's presence. I have, therefore, imagined characters who endure differing degrees of challenge, sadness, or suffering. But I pray my readers will patiently read on past the sorrow, anticipating the vicarious joy of entering into His presence with Nick, or Matt, or Timmy, or the young guilty sinner—and with all the others! No matter the intensity of the struggle, each character discovers powerful victory in this life's journey or transitions into ultimate victory—

into the King's eternal presence. Oh, to catch a glimpse of Him—for now and forever!

Our eyes cannot see; our ears cannot hear; our minds cannot grasp what He has prepared for us. His presence, wonderful beyond human comprehension, cannot be imagined.

Yet, my finite mind has tried to imagine the infinite. I wonder if He is chuckling over my weak attempts or if He is pleased that I worship Him in this manner. Perhaps both are true.

And so I ponder . . .

What will it be like, one day—to enter into His wondrous presence? To discern the nail prints on His hands and feet! To gaze into His eyes! Will He give us enough breath to endure the joy? Or will it be calm, sweet, natural?

Is it possible that He would bid us join Him upon a fragrant Galilean hillside, where we would repose at His feet—mesmerized—by eternal truth, goodness, grace, mercy, and love?

INTO HIS PRESENCE

Now and Forever

A JOURNEY TO A PROMISE

S he reached out and grasped the nail-scarred hand of the Maker of Rainbows; it was then she experienced the full measure of His Promise: "I HAVE PREPARED A PLACE FOR YOU, AND WHERE I AM, NOW YOU WILL BE ALSO."

FROM OUT OF THE ASHES—A NEW FLAME WOULD BURN

A strange and unexplainable comfort descended from another world beyond the stars, like a soft cooling mist, putting out a fire, wrapping itself around the man who now—truly had everything.

CRY VICTORY

It was then he told her of another perfect Prince that was slain . . . a Lamb who one day voluntarily walked into the jaws of an enemy that laughed. He told of a Father who cried and of a world that could live because the Lamb had died. "It's a fine thing to know this Lamb," he said.

TWO MIRACLES IN THE DESERT

Nick rose slowly, painfully, and stumbled toward Danny. He bent over his enemy, dropped to his knees, loosened the cover from his canteen, and drop by precious drop, trickled the warm liquid into his brother's coughing mouth.

GUILTY AS CHARGED

The little kid on the bike. A sob sneaked up on her. She hadn't meant to hit him. "I deserve whatever I get," she shouted silently within herself. No outward movement betrayed her desperation.

THE POWER OF LIGHT'S LOVE

On the saddest day of his life, in a strange place, with an unknown messenger, he had just made the most important and lasting commitment of his existence. Somehow he was aware that he was no longer alone.

A MESSAGE ON THE WIND

The loneliness nagged at her from within just as did the constant storm of questions. She knew by experience that life's most significant moments—pain, death, confrontation with truth—had to be faced alone.

THE CARPENTER'S SON

He brought her a small dog, a wiggly, black-eyed poodle with a friendly tail. "It's a baby I want. She ran to her bed and flung herself into its mute comfort. Her goose-down pillow was wet.

THE ROCK WHICH STOOD FIRM

Matt wiped his brow with a mud-streaked forearm. Fresh blood oozed from scrapes on his fingers and smudged his gray-tweed suit coat and trousers. He felt no pain for the moment; surprisingly, he felt no terror, only gripping fatigue. The astonishing events of the past few hours had numbed him.

ARMED AND READY TO SOAR

Lisa stifled a scream. She must not alert the enemy to their position. She clutched at David's sleeve, ripping faded cotton. He encircled her with muscular arms and pulled her face close into his chest. She sobbed silently.

A TREE NO STORM COULD CONQUER

The wind roared out of the north. The man and boy stood beneath the weeping willow and stared at the house below. The boy rested against the man and placed his hands also on the worn Bible, into which their spiritual roots had been planted deep and strong. The wind that blew at them without mercy would never be the conqueror.

A TREASURE IN HER GARDEN

A thousand lonely souls groveling in the dirt, stirred by the warming call of the Son, filled their empty places with her living Seed. Through the night her tears watered the earthly promise now nearly indiscernible in Grandma's old Bible, "... shall doubtless come again rejoicing."

IN THE BEGINNING

As the Eternal Word, gazing upon this precious creature, prepared to present him with a wife, only He was cognizant of just how precious man was and the price to be paid for his eternal freedom. The hissing serpent of undesignated origin slithered again through the open space under the Banyon tree.

WHEN THE TIME WAS RIGHT

He removed his golden crown. He stood before all in his humility. Yet they fell prone in worship, for not one in this place doubted for a moment his eternal worthiness. "It is time to finish this gate," was all He said.

. . . AND THEN THROUGH THE GATE

He transported her to the home He'd prepared. As they stood before the entrance, she looked first upon the gate and then upon her hand. Her pearl ring sparkled. Somehow it was the gate—adorned now for her, as for the most treasured of brides.

A Journey to the Promise

*From the rising of the sun unto the going down of the
same the Lord's name is to be praised.*

Psalm 113:3

Her hands were gnarled and tired, bruised, scarred, arthritic. They told a story and they held a promise. No, actually, they clung to a Promise. I GO TO PREPARE A PLACE FOR YOU, AND WHERE I GO THERE YOU MAY BE ALSO.

The story began seventy-eight years ago. The place was dark and warm and very safe. Da THUMP. Da THUMP. The soothing sound echoed endlessly into her consciousness. From afar, though, she heard many strange and fearful rumblings. Her little hands flung themselves as she sensed danger lurked somewhere. But her ever-rocking cradle eased her trembling. Her little, stubby fingers curled in peace.

Then suddenly a violent grip seized her everywhere and she gasped. "No!" screamed her little soul but it was a futile cry. Great jaws pushed and her little fingers grabbed in vain at nothingness. The terror ended as suddenly as it had begun.

Lovely sensations engulfed her—a gentle hand, a low coo, and a new mother's joyful, soothing tears soft upon her cheek. She sensed this was a far better place. This was a place prepared just for her. Her wrinkled, down-covered little fingers grasped her daddy's big, hairy, work-hardened ones and she heard him laugh. It was a promise of love, of protection—when the neighbor dog would growl low in his throat; when a marauding swarm of wasps would buzz close to her cascading curls; when a motorcycle would explode out of the darkness. How she would cling to Papa's hand—and that promise of safety from unknown dangers that lurked.

Time passed. No longer did she remember that first darkness. Sunshine and song and color filled her life. Rainbows and butterflies were everywhere. They adorned her bed, her walls, her mama's garden and her soul, for always she listened to the sound of laughter and often she heard the name Jesus. Mama and Daddy attached great significance to that name—as if it somehow held a Promise.

She reached for her toes and caught the elusive, little squiggly things and Mama's laughter echoed in her soul. She caught raindrops on her fingers and the opalescent sunbeams danced in her hair and Mama showed her colors in the sky. Little fingers reached to capture the iridescence. Papa and Mama laughed. "Jesus made the rainbow," they said, even though she was too young to understand."

Months passed. She grew. One day the longed-for treasure was finally hers—48 CRAYOLAS—grasped, more often broken. Chubby fingers painted rainbows of every size and description. Joyfully she hung them all on the refrigerator door. They all symbolized the Promise.

She loved the "Promise." Never again would a catastrophic flood destroy the earth. She loved the big word *catastrophic*.

Mama said it was a grownup word and Daddy laughed when she iterated "cas a sop ic"; therefore, she repeated it often. She began to understand that Daddy and Mama totally believed in the promises of Jesus. He made good promises. Mama and Daddy made her feel safe. The Promise made her feel safe.

The seasons passed; the rain fell; with every rainbow she again considered the Promise. It became a part of her—that Promise. Just like the butterflies, and the sunbeams, and the laughter, and the love in her parents' eyes.

She was growing up. She peered at her reflection. "A lovely rainbow of colors," she mused. "Light green on the lid, perhaps a touch of silver. Perfect. Magenta on the cheekbone, just below the pupil now, and rub just a dab of pink on the lips—purple nails with little butterflies applied. Very mod. A bit more red to highlight the ash-blond hair—too drab, really, to attract any discerning male." Well-manicured nails patted the extra fluff just over the ear. Intense scrutiny—and decision followed. "Lord, you created rainbows and I have created a mess." She laughed aloud as she grabbed a tissue.

Standing in the doorway, an adoring mother and father beamed. She turned and grinned at them. In the midst of their love stood the invisible Jesus.

Just a few times the great ball of heat rose above the horizon it seemed, and just a few fiery red farewells to the same, a few storms, and a few rainbows and then one day she stood in white on freshly cut grass. A new, strong hand offered her the promise of protection. Dad's big hand grasped the shoulder of this new man in her life. Mom held him tightly. Then mingling their tears with their laughter, her parents stepped aside.

Her heart met his, their hands clasped, and their lives became one. Together they reached out to the Maker of Rainbows and clung to Him. With her hand in her husband's, time stood still as she contemplated the magnitude of this moment.

Years passed. Dark clouds appeared, threatened, struck. One of Adam's race, she could not claim immunity from the clouds. Miscarriage, a home fire, a jangling call in the night— Dad was gone.

But the rainbows kept appearing. A little boy with green eyes, a little girl with cascading blond hair, a husband's faithfulness, a monarch butterfly performing a pirouette on the wind, the love songs of cardinals, the fragrance of spring lilacs, a perfect puffy omelet, the aroma of baking bread permeating her home, the satisfying usefulness of her hands—and best of all, the Promise—I GO TO PREPARE A PLACE FOR YOU.

Still, the years passed. The little boy and the little girl laughed and chased kittens and rainbows and butterflies. All the while she instilled in them a love for the Promise.

One bright, unclouded day on a freshly cut lawn, she clung to the hand of her husband as they listened to their daughter proclaim her own vow of love. They stepped aside, and through happy tears they saw the invisible, smiling Creator of Love with his arms wrapped around their child and her beloved, and they knew their son would soon do the same and they would again hold chubby fingers and hear belly laughs of many tow-headed little children and they would tell them also about rainbows and a Promise they could trust.

Then one day her husband took her hand in his. He searched her soul with his eyes. He reminded her of the Promise, for it was his Promise also. He would wait for her in a better land.

So…she said…goodbye. Often, next to his resting place she would sit in quiet repose. Once she opened misty eyes and saw a translucent butterfly—a prism radiant with color. Trusting her, it rested a moment upon her hand, seemed to kiss away her tears, seemed again to remind her of the Promise. Then it flitted easily toward Heaven. "Like his soul," she murmured.

She'd seen many clouds and many rainbows. Finally her time to claim the Promise drew near. As she grasped the silken sheet and pulled it to her wrinkled throat, she closed her eyes and beheld a rainbow more magnificent than any of earthly hues. Excited, she cooed, "It's beautiful."

Her daughter grasped her hand and caressed it softly. "What is, Mom?"

"The Promise. See. There on my bed." She paused, for a strange memory flooded her mind. "Once I didn't want to leave a dark, safe place. The process wasn't pleasant, My Dear. But there were your grandma and grandpa and music and flowers and rainbows and the Promise of Jesus. A far, far better place it was. A far, far better place awaits me again. A prepared place. I think I'm walking on the rainbow. I've always wanted to touch a rainbow."

She reached out and grasped the nail-scarred hand of the Maker of Rainbows; it was then she experienced the full measure of His Promise: "I HAVE PREPARED A PLACE FOR YOU, AND WHERE I AM, NOW YOU WILL BE ALSO."

Whereby are given unto us exceeding great and precious promises: that by these ye might be partakers of the divine nature.

II Peter 1:4

To our family's youngest—Peyton, Amelia, Brent, Caleb, Riley, Charis, Layla, John Daniel.
You have just begun the journey.
I pray that you, along with all the children in our family, will love the Promise.

From Out of the Ashes—A New Flame Would Burn

*But let all those that put their trust in thee rejoice: let
them ever shout for joy, because thou defendest them:
let them also that love thy name be joyful in thee.
For thou, Lord wilt bless the righteous . . .*

Psalm 5:11, 12

Michael poked at the blue flame with a bent pine twig.
The log disintegrated. Sparks rose in the wind, siz-

zled in the mountain air, and fell to an ashy grave unnoticed in the darkness.

The whimsical breeze whiffed the rolling smoke this way and that. He blinked the sting from his eyes. The fragrance of pine smoke embedded itself in his woolen shirt and beard.

"Yep. White wine, rich women, and the sweet song of the wild saxophone—that's all I need," Michael affirmed. "And throw in a metallic blue Corvette Stingray, maybe a few thoroughbreds for a touch of luxury."

Lyle laughed softly and shook his head. "And a mammoth house with a pool and Jacuzzi?"

Michael knew Lyle had never shared his love for fancy living. He laid another log gently across dwindling yellow tongues of flame. He opened the foil and poked his fork into the succulent pink meat of fresh brook trout sizzling in butter and lemon juice. It was definitely ready.

Every summer when they met for a week in the clean, Wyoming altitude, Michael recounted his accumulations and aspirations.

"I want to buy a private plane," he declared. "I'm taking flying lessons. Maybe next summer I'll come and pick you up from Seminary. Got a landing strip on your exercise field?"

Preoccupied, Lyle merely smiled and pensively watched the fire.

A bat zigzagged among the branches above them. From another campsite a small dog yipped excitedly. Old Jupiter raised his malamute head and peeked through squinty eyes, then rolled over and dozed, content in his cool nest of orange leaves.

Michael stared at blue flames consuming pinewood. Into the fire he absently threw a dry leaf, an aspen twig, a trout skeleton. The fire crackled. A puff of pine smoke tickled his nostrils. He flipped a piece of cellophane toward the flame. How quickly it vanished, even before it contacted the log below. Here, then gone. The flame gobbled everything, spitting and belching in its greediness. For a long time the fire burned, until only a glow emanated from below a charred, empty log.

Lyle had been unusually quiet all week, never broaching the subject. Michael knew he would have to bring it up.

In the crisp, autumn air, they sat by the edge of the lapping lake and listened to the voices of the night. Jupiter edged in and plopped between them.

"How's your dad?" Michael finally asked.

"Bad. Probably a matter of weeks, maybe less." Lyle stared at the path of reflected light inching imperceptibly toward them on the dark water.

"I've been so busy." Michael cleared his throat. A frog croaked in perfect mimicry. "Next week, I'll get down for sure. You know he's been my father, too. All those years he raised me . . . I—I'll help with the bills." He stammered himself out of words. The frogs continued to bar-oop their empty promises into the night air.

Jupiter looked at the two men he loved, both solemn with human emotion. He laid his huge head on Michael's knee and thumped his tail.

A meteor raced its fiery path into the horizon and sizzled into nothingness.

Michael buried his fingertips in the dog's thick coat and massaged the layers of rolling skin below, insulating him from cold and pain. The dog grinned at him, panting even in night's coolness.

He glanced sidelong at Lyle, his cousin; for most of his life more like his younger brother. He swallowed hard. Lyle's eyes were shut. Michael wanted to talk, to prattle in nostalgia, or perhaps to plead again for a business partnership, or even to talk of Lyle's God.

"The God you serve has no need of me." Michael wondered why he said it. He put his head in his hands. Guilt wrapped itself around him and strangled. He felt utterly desolate. The week had been a bummer.

Lyle patted Jupiter's head, rested his hand for a moment on Michael's shoulder, and departed to his tent.

Michael shivered and moved closer to Jupiter. Monday he hoped to close the deal on the estate he'd been eyeing. It would take more negotiation, but the effort would be well worth it. He loved the game of real estate: the seeking, the baiting, the winning. The house was vacant; he'd move in immediately. He pictured his horses running freely in the adjoining rich pasture.

A dark cloud floated above the lake. Jupiter growled at an unknown nocturnal creature scurrying in the undergrowth. A mosquito whined close to his ear, incognito in the darkness.

Lyle's father surely would understand. Only a week longer. It wouldn't matter so much. He couldn't chance losing this deal. The house alone was worth a small fortune more than they were asking. He swatted angrily at the mosquito.

Drops of rain roused the ever-sleepy dog. Michael stood and looked sadly into the darkness, the rain chilling his body. It seemed anticlimactic—the end of this week—somehow destined to offer only rain and the chill of grief and the burning cold of guilt.

He tossed fitfully in his tent. Once in the night Jupiter stood and howled mournfully. By sunrise a drizzle had settled in.

As they packed their gear and hoisted their white canoe atop Lyle's weather-beaten, old van, Michael sensed this departure as uniquely significant. He wondered why. Subdued, he reflected silently upon the imminence of death. Lyle's father would soon be gone. Was this the reason for his melancholy— a premonition?

*

In silence they drove down and around the winding switch-backs, looking out thousands of feet into the green patchwork below. The sunlight flickered ever-new pathways among the cloud shadows. "Nothing in life is static," Michael mumbled. Reality and destiny waited patiently below.

*

"It must have been the bad weather," Michael reflected as he swiftly maneuvered his metallic blue Stingray around the winding, rural asphalt leading to his new home. "That's why I was depressed last weekend." He accelerated, relishing the surge of instant power at his command. Drunk with the wine of success, he whizzed euphorically through the autumn afternoon.

He moved the Corvette through the open, spiked, iron gate admitting him to his newly-acquired estate, squealed around the final bend, and came to a screeching halt. It was then his breath stopped.

Parked under the large oak was Lyle's old white van. Rust was eroding the metal around the gas tank and over the rear right window. A front tire was low. Lyle sat in silence on the step, his arms buried in Jupiter's animal comfort.

The funeral was to be held the following Monday.

Through the afternoon and into the twilight, Lyle and Michael reminisced of past times: of summer evenings with Pop laughing at them while they squealed with joy over each new fish on the line; of Pop patiently waiting while they argued over who would carry out the garbage and who would wash dishes; of the day when Pop first brought home a Bible and awkwardly explained that a new passion burned within his soul; of the day Lyle also understood.

As the darkness of guilt deepened within him, Michael wandered through the spacious rooms, silent as a specter among the night shadows. Guilt and emptiness tormented him. Lyle's final words that evening haunted him. "I'll see Pop again. Will you?"

He walked out into the night under a starless sky, and where colts had frolicked that day, he sat in damp grass. He looked back at his pillared mansion where Lyle slept, wrapped in a comfort sent from another world far beyond the cloud-darkened stars.

A grayness moved out of night's opaqueness and licked his hand. "You're always with me, aren't you, Old Boy? Like Lyle's God is always with him. Only someday YOU also will be gone..."

The man who had everything buried his face in his dog's thick fur and wept.

Suddenly Jupiter began to bark frantically. Michael jumped to his feet. Fear slashed at him from every direction. Agony silently screamed from his soul. He'd never known such paralyzing terror.

Helpless, he stood there, gaping. Gigantic tongues of laughing, mocking heat within his villa consumed the only living human he had always loved—Lyle, from whom he'd not yet begged forgiveness.

The mourning howl of distant sirens penetrated his consciousness. A neighbor, seeing the glow, must have called for help. Michael could not breathe. His frozen brain would command no movement. Long after the rescuers had left, he sat shivering in the field, clinging to Jupiter. Nobody had seen him there.

The sun's morning rays played happily in the rolling clouds, oblivious to the man sitting in the clutches of sorrow. Finally, urged by Jupiter, he stumbled toward the ruins and kicked his way through the ashes. Some areas still felt warm. The fire had mocked his priorities with uncompromising effectiveness.

He stumbled to the place where Lyle had slept. Very little was even remotely recognizable. Then he stopped, his attention riveted upon a miracle.

Lying in the ashes was a Book only partly charred, its pages fluttering softly in the early morning breeze. Upon it lay a picture—a photograph he remembered well—of Lyle and his father, and of Jupiter as a pup, and of him. He grasped it in amazement. Still poignant from the mouth of Lyle, words circled in red upon the pages of the Book unburned by the all-consuming fire reached out and whispered softly to him. "Seek ye first the kingdom of God . . ."

Michael read the message through blurred eyes.

He dropped to his knees. "Lord, I don't know if you need me or not, but I need you."

Jupiter moved in close, whimpering, nuzzling, always approving.

A strange and unexplainable comfort descended from another world beyond the stars, like a soft cooling mist, putting out a fire, wrapping itself around the man who now—truly had everything.

> *Then said I, Woe is me! For I am undone;*
> *because I am a man of unclean lips,*
> *and I dwell in the midst of a people of unclean lips:*
> *for mine eyes have seen the King, the Lord of hosts.*
> *Then flew one of the seraphims unto me,*
> *having a live coal in his hand,*
> *which he had taken with the tongs from off the altar:*
> *And he laid it upon my mouth, and said,*
> *Lo this hath touched thy lips;*
> *and thine iniquity is taken away, and thy sin purged.*

Isaiah 6:5-7

Dedicated to Tim—son, who loved the Wyoming campfire, the sizzling trout, the big dog panting by his side, my precious son who in so many ways could speak of miracles.

Cry Victory

Be glad in the Lord,
and rejoice, ye righteous:
and shout for joy,
all ye that are upright in heart.

Psalm 32:11

He lay there, tiny, wet, and shivering. As his mother licked the joy of love into his nostrils, he began the struggle toward life.

A little girl absorbed in nativity gazed, suspended in time, breathless. This lamb was to be hers, a gift from Papa. Papa had written her a certificate of ownership in fancy letters. All that remained was to fill in the name—when she had chosen it—in the special space reserved for that very purpose.

He lifted his tiny head, so vulnerable to cold and death. But the lamb's thoughts were on life, not death. Struggling, he rose; wobbling, he lifted his head and bleated in a clear warble, "Vic-tor-y!"

Papa moved in close, praising gently, soothing the hovering ewe. She stomped her foot in motherly agitation. His hands moved on her newly shorn back, giving confidence, and then the baby was in his arms, nudging eagerly, searching Papa's sleeves for sustenance. Papa smiled. "He's strong. I can find no fault in him. He's a perfect lamb. A little Prince."

Deep within the child's awareness, an eternal truth awakened—to possess a lamb was a fine thing—the finest of privileges.

As the little creature nestled naturally into his mother's rich provision and drank his first meal, her maternal instinct grunted and nudged and licked and urged. Watching every move, the little girl on her papa's knee also drank the fullness of life.

"Here, sit in the hay," her papa offered. He placed the new little Prince close. In instant affinity the lamb tumbled toward her and nuzzled his animal fragrance into her heart and neither noticed nor cared that a withered, useless arm hung shamefully from her right shoulder.

An object of derision, that little remnant of what should have been often subjected her to ridicule. Some children had not yet learned the real source of human worth.

As the lamb laid his softness upon her shame, a tingling warmth spread upward, ending at the deepest place in her heart. There in her arms, tired from his dramatic entrance into the realities of this planet, he fell asleep. She sat motionless, memorizing every aspect of his perfection.

She longed to shout to taunters everywhere. "Don't look at me or my silly ole' arm ever again. Look at my beautiful lamb. Then you can love me as I love my lamb.

Spring celebrated its arrival with silent explosions of blossoms. Everywhere little buds stretched out beyond their greenness, yawning with the awakening of the new season.

The snow melted from the mountain that towered majestically over their valley. Little streams of icy blueness sparkled down the mountain, and the earth gulped its offering.

School hours moved slowly. She lived in those moments of lengthening shadows when she and Prince would romp through the low places where the mountain flowers and the patches of wild blueberries beckoned. With endless games of their own imagination, their little legs would fly joyfully, only occasionally kissing the earth, the child calling for her Prince and laughing, simply because in her life—there was a lamb. Responsive always, full of vigor, he became her happy shadow. Both inhaled the freshness of the mountain air and the delicious joy of their mutual devotion.

Each day at twilight her tiny fingers squeezed and tugged at the udder of the patient old black and white Holstein cow until, resigned, the bovine relented and into a glass bottle there flowed warm, white froth.

The lamb stood waiting, bleating happily, until the nippled bottle had been readied. Vigorously he pulled, as he gulped the warm milk, until she could barely hold it with one little hand. "Another good arm would help," she muttered. Then as he nuzzled his nose into her tummy, nothing mattered except the love of this lamb.

As dark intruded upon each day's frolic, Papa carefully secured the gates and doors of the animal shelter. Urgently the child inspected his work. For on the chilling winds of night often came the hungry wail of the great mountain catamount. Though she had never seen the sharp-clawed lion of the heights, she pictured him in her imagination. Long and bronze, with piercing green eyes, he would hypnotize his prey while his tail rhythmically swished, propelling him forward. Then she would see his teeth, pointed and sharp, descending upon her weakness. In the night she would scream.

Papa's arms were around her. "He only roams at night. The sheep are locked in. They are safe. We are safe." His voice caressed her terror.

*

As the blossoms of spring burst forth into full maturity of summer, the child played long, happy hours. With Prince at her side, she ventured farther and farther up the mountain in search of golden dandelions. "I will make you a crown, my Prince," she promised.

She sat in the midst of a large golden patch of dandelions. Finishing a glistening, woven crown, she called the lamb and placed it upon his head. Off he bounced to the next hill, lapping up the joy of her love. She lay happily on the green mountain carpet and counted fluffy cumulus lambs in the sky.

She rolled over to search the hill for a four-leaf clover, resting her chin upon her good hand. Suddenly her little heart began to thump out of control. There only a few feet away grinned the object of all her nightmares, swishing his hypnotic tail, gurgling death deep in his throat. She sat up, startled by fear, her limp arm clutched pathetically to her side. The other flung itself in a futile movement to protect her face. The huge menace stalking her moved with deliberate purpose. She sank into the grass in sheer terror, paralyzed.

Suddenly bounding from the nearby hill came a frantic lamb bleating his gentle cry. Straight at the big mountain cat he ran, his little black heels flashing in the sunlight. The golden crown still adorned his head.

Distracted from the child, the lion turned away and roared his laugh of brutal death. A leap, a mighty claw raised, and the bleating was silenced. Forever. A grief too great for words clutched at the child's throat, strangling her breath.

The lion once again turned his focus upon her. As his upper lip rose in arrogance, a piece of once-white, blood-stained wool dropped from the corner of his mouth.

Suddenly a bullet whistled past her head and lodged in a white birch tree. In a flash of sunlight, the mountain cat disappeared into the protective darkness of quaking aspens and evergreens.

Her papa was holding her close. His cheeks were wet; his throat moved strangely up and down. Together they stared at the remains of love.

She squirmed out of Papa's grasp and picked up the crown woven of dandelions, designed with great care for a Prince.

Papa dug a hole and placed the broken sacrifice within. They knelt beside the tiny grave. Papa tried to say beautiful words, but his voice cracked. On a stone next to a tall tree, he scratched the words: "My Prince." She laid the crown upon the dirt. She knew that she lived because her lamb had died.

She didn't know how long they sat there clinging to each other. Finally Papa picked her up and strode down the mountain toward the sunset. From over his shoulder, through blurred eyes she watched the place of despair fade in the distance. "Good bye, my Prince."

*

As the days slowly ticked by, and the months, and the years, the little girl learned to look upon others with a rare compassion. To those who sought pleasure in chiding her, she responded with sympathy, recognizing their great need. In a wisdom born of sorrow, she understood that they sought worth. Sadly, they had never possessed a lamb.

The time came when a gentle man held the withered arm and tenderly kissed the shriveled finger stubs, for he looked within her soul and recognized great beauty.

One day she took him to the place where a tiny marker still said, "My Prince."

It was then he told her of another perfect Prince that was slain, a Man who walked on mountains and in valleys, a Lamb who one day voluntarily walked into the jaws of an enemy that laughed. He told of a Father who cried and of a world that could live because the Lamb had died. "It's a fine thing to know this Lamb," he said.

And then he gently turned her so that her eyes would not focus on that place of sorrow. "'Victory" was his death cry. But we shall see this Lamb again. You see, it was also His resurrection cry!"

She remembered a tiny creature struggling in the cold.

He continued. "His voice echoes upon these snowy peaks and into every valley and deeper still into the depth of ever human heart."

Standing there, her vision blurred. She turned and gazed again at the little hill where long ago death had stabbed her tiny soul. On that little grave she saw a cross. Below the innocent sufferer lay a mangled, blood-stained robe—made of white lamb's wool. She heard a mighty voice commanding her to be whole.

Irresistibly compelled by love, she knelt in green velvet. Puffy clouds frolicked playfully above her. She looked up and proclaimed the victory cry, "Worthy, worthy is the lamb that was slain to receive power and riches and wisdom and strength and honor and glory and blessing."

While the birds joyously whirled their accompaniment, the young couple stood hand in hand, and together rehearsed the song they would sing with the multitudes before the throne. "Blessing and honor and glory and power be unto Him that sitteth upon the throne, and unto the Lamb forever."

In a nearby pasture a flock grazed contentedly. A tiny lamb raised his head, listened to the song, and bleated in affirmation, "Baa-a-men!"

> *He was oppressed, and he was afflicted,*
> *yet he opened not his mouth:*
> *he is brought as a lamb to the slaughter.*

Isaiah 53:7

Dedicated to Theodore, my father, who gave me
orphaned lambs to mother.

At 91 you met the Lamb of God; at 93 you entered
into His presence.

Two Miracles in the Desert

O God, thou art my God;
early will I seek thee: my soul thirsteth for thee,
my flesh longeth for thee in a dry and thirsty land,
where no water is . . .

Psalm 63:1

"It's all your fault! Your fault!"

Red with rage, he stumbled across the sand while the relentless eye of the sun followed every lurching step.

Squinting in its merciless glare, he turned to look at his younger brother. He blinked, fighting nausea and delirium. A cyclonic dust swirl whipped needle-like particles into his brows and nostrils.

He felt his strength languishing, dissipating with his sweat. His mind was playing games with him. His skull throbbed as he tried to remember what had happened. With repulsion he glared at his half-brother who staggered behind him in the oppressive heat of the Mojave Desert.

As the great ball of fire apathetically rolled westward, he considered an old terror, born anew, a phobia conceived in fever and pain and a stark hospital room. "Another bite like this and you're a gonner," Doc had cautioned. His allergy made him vulnerable. It was the marauding scorpion he feared, more than the dark empty night, more than the shimmy of endless tongues of heat lapping methodically at his being.

His loathing for his brother grew. This ill-omened venture over an alien wasteland had been Danny's obsession.

"Get up, you . . . worthless . . . quitter. We've got to keep walking!" He grabbed Danny by the collar and jerked him upright.

Trudging through the granuled eternity, he mused. Wet, wet waves splashing, transparent on cool evening beaches. Mindy, the girl he loved, cooing and laughing in the moonlight.

Tears welled up. With a grimy shirt, he wiped them away, coughing and choking. His brother would never detect his weakness. Never!

"We should have stayed with the copter," Danny gasped. Then he stumbled and fell to his knees. "Nick, I need water."

Fists clenched, jaw tight, Nick towered above the one he'd long despised. In truth, he wanted Danny to die. Danny had always been the favored one, the love child of his mother and stepfather, while he—Nick—had wandered aimlessly in a desert of loneliness, at least until Mindy.

Now his opportunity for revenge smiled seductively as it enticed him, tickled his mind with temptation.

Sweat glistened on Danny's skin, pale with heat exhaustion. Irregular, shallow breathing proclaimed to Nick that Danny was in serious trouble. Indecision skipped dishonorably over the landscape and planted its feet firmly in front of him.

He closed his eyes tightly and heard Mindy's voice pleading in the distance. "If any man thirst, let him come unto me and drink." Where was Mindy? He couldn't remember.

He nudged her words from his consciousness and grasped his nearly empty canteen. He checked the screw-on cover; it was secure. Though weak-kneed, he stood up shakily and scanned nearby sand dunes for saguaro cactus. Its fluted stem, swelled during rain, would have stored moisture, not much, but enough to save his life. None were in sight. He would not squander his precious water.

Only his desire to be controlled in Danny's presence checked his hysteria. His vision blurred momentarily. He plopped in the sand. Its unwelcome heat penetrated his khaki trousers.

A kangaroo rat scooted across the sand and paused, eyeing Nick cautiously, listening for the low, drumming sound of his family in the burrow.

Nick glared at the rat. Mournfully, he lamented, "Your own body changes food to liquid, while I weaken, and wither, and simply wait to die." Nick choked on the final, irrefutable words. His resentment flaring, he wailed: "You don't need water, do you, you ugly, rotten, vermin-infested rodent!" His shrill accusation sent the rat scurrying across the shifting dunes.

He tried to focus on Mindy. He envisioned her gliding through the depths of her father's Olympic pool—sleek, slim, beautiful, smiling. But as she broke the surface of his thoughts, she was speaking. "He that believeth on me, as the Scripture hath said, out of his belly shall flow rivers of living water."

In the distance, the airwaves bubbled and shimmied. A gigantic waterfall cascaded over verdant mountain cliffs. Mindy rode the falls, a mermaid in innocence, beckoning him into its green transparency. He heard high-pitched laughter and careened around awkwardly to confront the intruder.

"Nick," Danny groaned with a thick, whispered voice. "Why—are you—laughing?"

Nick scowled. The spraying, bubbling waterfall, and Mindy, and the maniacal intruder vanished. Instead to his horror, he saw only the wreckage of the downed helicopter, a tangled pile of twisted ebony iron.

He thought of a cool, summer shower, with round succulent drops of wetness on his face, on his arms, on the cool green grass, and Mindy in his embrace.

He grabbed his perishing brother and dragged him roughly, haltingly, to the shade of the helicopter. In a lucid moment, he recognized the full circle of their tracks. He fell, crunching his head against the bent iron leg under the pilot's seat. He scanned the wreckage for scorpions. In the heat he shivered.

The dead radio lay flung to the ground during the crash, mocking his mortality. He crawled to it and flipped the buttons. In fury he threw the useless box, emitting an animal groan from fuzzy lips. Sweat oozed from his skin, burning his eyes with salt. He was breathing hard. He lay with his ear and cheek embedded in the sand. From a great distance he heard Mindy, " . . . shall never thirst." He clung to the buckskin canteen, hoarding the treasure within.

Danny groaned in the shade under the belly of the machine.

Nick turned away. His head ached, like a searing hot iron was jamming into his skull above the left temple. The droplets of sweat irritated him. He grimaced as he wiped the sogginess. There upon his hand, blood streaked the sweat. For the first time he realized he had been injured, how seriously he had no way of knowing.

He snorted bitterly at the irony. He could use a little of Mindy's everlasting water—a canteen full of it would do for a start.

Mindy was like him, an outcast, a victim also of a broken home. But unlike him, she had healed. Always telling him about some everlasting river.

She floated before him, seemed to be sitting in a sky-blue, gently-flowing stream. Nick tried to force this vision from his thoughts, but there his Mindy sat washing blood from her face and her shoulder, washing and laughing in the azure coolness.

Beside him, Danny drifted in and out of consciousness.

Despondently Nick bemoaned his brother's existence, his venom dissipated by a sweltering wind gust. "I've always hated you, you know. And now, while you die, I'm going to drink this water—and live!"

Danny didn't respond. His lips were thick. Sand flies settled on the cracks and blisters. Danny did not move.

A lone, black scavenger circled ominously above. Gathering strength, Nick struggled to a kneeling position, scooped a handful of sand, and flung it at nature's garbage collector.

"Take him, not me, him—you hear?" The orbit of the bird was unaffected.

Nick slipped to the ground and weakly roared his frustration.

The unrelenting sun watched with its disinterested eye. A second pair of black wings, expending little effort, joined its companion and circled patiently.

Mindy's loveliness haunted his dizziness. "This day shall you be with me in Paradise," she murmured. "The thief on the cross only had to ask."

His temples throbbed erratically. Cotton exploded in his throat, choking, expanding. Wind and sun had pitilessly attacked his face, streaking it red. Vermillion trickles of blood drying on his left temple splotched the smooth texture above his brown beard.

A scorpion scampered confidently across his boot. He watched it without moving. It flipped itself onto the sand. With a hollow stare, he clutched the canteen and gazed out over the gigantic graveyard. The only sign of life was the dead tumbleweed, rolling and undirected, pushed hither and thither by every puff of wind.

He remembered Mindy's gentle words: "The thief on the cross only had to ask." He pondered her confidence in those words, the sweetness of her eyes as she waited for his response.

A small, black Book suddenly invited his attention. He wondered why Mindy's Book lay directly in front of him. He stared at it long and hard—hard and long.

"I, too, am a thief." Soundlessly his lips acknowledged the truth. "I've robbed every life I've touched." Staring at Danny, he struggled for coherent thought. He heard the faraway sound of his own lungs wheezing, cells clamoring for oxygen, for life.

"The thief on the cross only had to ask." Mindy's heartfelt entreaty echoed in his memory.

His need for survival eased itself into second priority. Within his soul an old battle of eternal consequence raged— until into Nick there flowed awareness . . . surrender . . . release.

He rose slowly, painfully, and stumbled toward Danny. Nick bent over his enemy, dropped to his knees, loosened the cover from his canteen, and drop by precious drop, trickled the warm liquid into his brother's coughing mouth.

"Lord, in your name—I give this water—to my brother. Take me this day to Paradise."

He watched Danny respond, open his eyes, forgive.

Nick slumped to the ground and rested his head upon hot sand. He closed his eyes. He was smiling.

Then he felt it. Cold, clear water tumbling over his hair, his chest, his legs. He lay back while the splashy coolness flowed over his body. He heard the clear, melodic ring of Mindy's laugh. There she was, the girl he loved, bounding toward him.

His head no longer hurt. His dizziness seemed gone forever, replaced by tranquility, like the river Mindy always spoke of—somehow, eternal.

Then she was by his side. "Nick!" How easily she pulled him up and to her, how jubilantly. A crown of sapphires rested in her curls. He touched her face. The blood was gone, the wound healed.

Suddenly—she fell prone beside him.

A melody like stars singing and a sweetness like incense surrounded him. A breeze caressed his soul. The sound of living water that had refreshed millions surged about him.

Thrilled, unable to comprehend the rapture, he turned in awestruck wonder.

Mindy was laying her crown before the One who had poured the water of life into the parched dryness of her being. A wondrous fountain called joy sprung out of Nick, yet bittersweet, for he, perhaps just like the thief on the cross, had no crown to offer.

The One who loved the thief moved in quietness and reclined beside him. Nick's eyes mesmerized by Majesty, broke away only as *HE* nodded Nick's attention into swirling clouds. With His touch they parted. Nick's breath stopped as he witnessed the incredible scene below.

A helicopter, a snarl of iron. Two bodies, one a beautiful girl named Mindy, impaled upon metal within the machine, dry blood on her face and shoulder. Lying like stone in the sand, his own form was covered in sand flies. A scorpion scampered on his elbow just below his rolled-up sleeve. Most amazing, there sat Danny, reading the small leather Book, which had ejected from Mindy's purse in the impact.

A gray cloud floated in from nowhere and hovered above the man sitting cross-legged in the heat. As the Great One closed His eyes for but a moment, a spark of lightning ignited the water. Great pellets of life-giving wetness rushed to the earth and enveloped the man. Danny rolled onto his back catching the torrent in his arms, in his mouth, laughing as the rain revived his strength.

With the Book grasped in his hand, Danny looked up through the rain to the cloud, seeming with more than his eyes to penetrate beyond its mystery. Then he spoke.

"Lord, two miracles—this incredible cloud—Danny choked as he stood and looked down at Nick's still form—and my brother gave me water. I, too, believe."

Nick felt a gentle weight upon his head. He reached up and removed the crown glimmering with sapphires. He looked at it a long, lingering, comprehending moment. Ten thousand winged voices swirled in perfect joy until the jeweled stones of the City's foundations seemed also to vibrate in eternal approval. Upon transparent gold Nick placed the sparkling crown at the King's feet.

The Lord God touched Nick with nail-scarred hands, looked into his eyes with incomprehensible love, and spoke eternal truth. "I am the resurrection and the life. He that believeth in me, though he were dead, yet shall he live."

The thief who had asked, Mindy who had beseeched, Nick who had finally understood, and Danny who had forgiven—all tasted the sweet water of redemption—the precious, freely-given water of eternal life.

Jesus answered and said unto her,
whosoever drinketh of this water shall thirst again:
but whosoever drinketh of the water that I shall give
him shall never thirst;
but the water that I shall give him shall be in him a
well of water
springing up into everlasting life.

John 4:13, 14

Dedicated to Michele—niece.
I vividly remember your phone call.
"I have supped freely of the Living Water" was the message.
"Bob and I have accepted Christ. I know this will please you."
Such a master of understatement are you!

Guilty as Charged

But the Lord shall endure forever:
he hath prepared his throne for judgment.
and he shall judge the world in righteousness,
he shall minister judgment to the people in uprightness.
The Lord also will be a refuge for the oppressed,
a refuge in times of trouble.
And they that know thy name will put their trust in thee:
for thou, Lord hast not forsaken them that seek thee.

Psalm 9:7-11

She'd been hauled in before by the flashing blue light and the grim-faced officer who now leaned against an aged pillar at the back of the courtroom. He was twirling his thumbs and staring at the ceiling.

On her forehead a stray, blond wisp drooped limply. She sat motionless, encased in regret. This time the offense demanded more consideration. Driving under the influence. No license. The little kid on the bike. Nobody told her if he had died. She yearned to ask. Instead she sat straight and set her jaw in ostentatious defiance.

From the courtroom and beyond echoed the babbling hum of a great crowd of spectators. Her case had instantly captured the interest of the public. A minor, obviously guilty. How would the judge dispense justice this time? The world wondered and waited.

The somber eyes of George Washington reproved her from his portrait on otherwise barren walls. She avoided his stare.

From the huge oak door behind the bench, the public accuser strutted in, looking self-assured. "An open and shut case," he'd proclaimed confidently to the press. The cliché in the newspaper made her swallow hard, but the lump in her throat seemed to be rolling in petroleum jelly.

The courtroom was rapidly filling to capacity. A thousand wondering eyes pierced her body, like newly sharpened arrows prepared for an execution.

"Mama," cried the concealed, despondent child within her. But Mama was sleeping off her own private despair somewhere in an obscure, darkened motel room, clutching in a brown bottle her liquid escape—her certain destruction.

The little kid on the bike. A sob sneaked up on her. She hadn't meant to hit him. "I deserve whatever I get," she shouted silently within herself. No outward movement betrayed her desperation.

The red-haired public defender glanced at her. His right eye twitched. Like a self-important chanticleer strutting around the barnyard, he would be the first to flee when the wolf approached. He was no match for the ferocious enemy across the aisle wagging his finger at her in bitter denunciation. Her witless attorney bobbed his head a few times and then squawked, "I can offer you no real cause for hope."

She eyed the immense portal, looming like a gigantic tomb behind the bench of justice. It led to the place of incarceration. There were only two doors in this room of public trial. One or the other would embrace this helpless representative of humanity, who shivered under the glaring lights of scrutiny.

Prison. There'd be no deliverance. She would be alone, a mere child subject to all the terrors conceived by evil minds. Prison. A place for mangling the body, mauling the soul.

"Father," cried the anguish within her. But Mama had taken her far away from him, deserting him long ago. His hands—her only memory—were badly scarred from a bike accident when just a child. The driver had been intoxicated. The realization renewed, it smacked her lungs, clubbing away residual air. She gasped for oxygen.

The clangor in the courtroom reverberated into her skull as if a retributive bass drummer had entered and stood within, throbbing the vibrations ever louder and faster.

A thousand little petitioning hands reached out of her mind seeking comfort, but found stability only in the invisible iron bars which enclosed her soul. A great torrent of tears released themselves within. She consciously controlled her breathing, but her desperate heart, like a ticking bomb, prepared to scatter fragments of her broken body into the darkness called infinity.

"You're a stoic one," clucked the inept man filling out the final details on her deposition. "Don't you delinquents ever FEEL anything?"

A sudden hush startled her. The multitude rose to acknowledge the authority of the judge. His presence filled the courtroom even before he spoke. He was acclaimed for fairness. Yet his verdicts, rendered with finality, allowed no appeals. The guilty had to satisfy the full penalty of the law.

Rising, she clutched the table before her, her fingers turning white with the pressure. Dizziness grabbed her brain and twisted it like children spinning a play-ground merry-go-round and around and around and her whole life spun off in tiny bits of fragmented film upon a gigantic high-definition television screen for all the murmuring spectators to behold; indeed, for the viewing of the whole world. Every thought, word, and action stood naked, revealed to all. She cringed in shame, mesmerized by the twisted bitterness of the flashing images.

The whirring machine slowed and quieted. A moan of sorrow arose from the accusing audience behind her, for there in still-frame she stood gazing down at a small boy lying on the road with hands mutilated in bicycle spokes, blood trickling from the corners of his mouth. The memory of his mother's wail pierced her eardrums.

Her inept defense attorney, the rooster, nudged her forward to stand before the huge oak podium—she a tiny, insignificant bit of protoplasm bowed in desperation.

From the corners of the Hall of Justice and from the world beyond she heard the word again and again: "Guilty, GUILTY, G U I L T Y." The crescendo rose until she herself was uttering, "Guilty. I am truly guilty."

She stood with bowed head, arms hung loose, the reality of her situation crushing her from every direction, those invisible iron bars moving ever closer and closer. Body, soul, and spirit—she was doomed.

Eyeing her with an angry scowl, his teeth glistening, the accuser came forward and howled above the cacophony. "Your h-honor." He stuttered noticeably over those words of respect. "You've seen the evidence. Of all things forbidden, despised by the law, she is guilty. Lying, thieving, murdering ..." With every accusation his eyes seemed to burn with an eerie, fiery light while his grin leered broader.

The judge shuffled her papers, looked at her intently, and considered her papers again.

The district attorney continued to whine.

Ignoring him, the judge spoke with incredible sadness. "How do you plead?"

"Guil-ty." She choked on the inevitable answer.

Instantly the giant screen lit up again; every lie, every blasphemy, every murderous thought flashed, confirming. With each picture the throng behind her roared with the new evidence, the dissonance of sounds intensifying into a mighty wail of anger.

The judge rose to his feet to proclaim sentence. He appeared to be floating in a vaporous cloud. She could see only his bearded face and the all-encompassing sadness in his eyes as he looked into hers. His voice, very loud and very near, reverberated past the cloud into unseen galaxies.

"You must be sentenced according to the law. Though the child you hit has not died, you have brought great pain. We cannot ignore your long record of crimes against the hearts of men. You are—guilty."

With the word, lightning flashed from his eyes and thundered into the recesses of her brain, echoing again into those distant galaxies and beyond. The cloud whirled and darkened until its blackness dumped torrential tears upon the earth. "GUILTY—seven years or $7000—GUILTY."

In the pocket of her skirt jingled $6.66. She had not the resource to purchase her own freedom.

From his seat, the D.A. cackled with victory; the sound forced its way into every shuddering soul.

The courtroom roared. The crowed writhed. The accuser stood at his post screaming with maniacal laughter. A bailiff opened the big, oak door, from which emanated a blinding, red glow. Two grinning guards with large, looped chains appeared. The accuser pointed at her and hopped up and down gleefully. The chicken darted away to bury himself within the crowd, lest he, too, be taken.

The towering judge majestically extended his arms up and out. Silence descended upon the expectant room. With deliberate movements, the judge unbuttoned the fastener on his black gown of authority. Sadly, he smoothed it as he laid it upon the antiquated, wooden podium, for he would wear it again. His imposing eyes compelled the riveted attention of every spectator. A silent, waiting world held its breath.

As the judge moved around the bench, he seemed suddenly frail. She wondered why he was wearing dusty sandals. He stood beside her and on his outstretched hands were thousand-dollar bills—seven of them, crisp, fresh, sufficient.

She stared at the hands offering redemption. They were mangled and scarred. In great body-wrenching sobs, she sank to her knees. "Father."

Invisible iron bars exploded into a million pieces and landed in a heap upon the head of the sullen district attorney, pouting, slinking out of the courtroom. Snarling in defeat, he was already immersed in his next case.

"Through all the dark and lonely places of this planet, I've been searching for you, My Child—ever since your mother took you away. I've been searching for her also."

Her tears cascaded upon His feet. Through bleary eyes she observed them to be bruised from the stones and briars, the eternal reminder of His agonizing search.

His love permeated every part of her. "You'll never be alone again. Neither death, nor life, nor angels, nor principalities, nor powers, nor things present, nor things to come, nor height, nor depth, nor any other creature shall separate you from Me."

She knew that what He said was true.

Multitudes turned in anger and followed the district attorney from the courtroom.

Just a few, those who had walked a narrow road to get there, remained. They stood in reverent silence, acutely aware that they too were guilty as charged, for they too had stood before this Judge, had faced His righteous justice, and had experienced His amazing grace.

Here and there a child, a man, a woman, focused on the beauty of those marred, outstretched hands and scarred feet, and began to sing in the sweet harmony of the guilty ones forever acquitted, forever set free. These were the ones who, along with her, had truly entered into His presence.

For we must all appear before the judgment seat of Christ;
that every one may receive the things done in the body,
for he hath made him to be sin for us,
who knew no sin,
that we might be made the righteousness of God in Him.

II Corinthians 6:10, 21

Dedicated to every member of Adam's race.

The Power of Light's Love

He brought them out of darkness
and the shadow of death,
and brake their bands in sunder.

Psalm 107:14

Darkness penetrated everything. It was the night of the new moon when the earth sits in space, one side of its heavy body shrouded in mammoth blackness, oblivious to the sun's brilliance and sustenance.

On the precipice he stood alone, suspended in time, balancing on the edge with nothingness below and all around. The darkness encompassed him fully—neither his eyes nor his heart perceived even the tiniest particle of light.

The melancholic notes of the organ dirge had vibrated their last sounds into space, leaving only the silent memory of dirt plopping in finality on two rectangular wooden boxes.

He had fled to the mountain at dusk. The great ball of fire in the western sky had eased itself out of his awareness. His eyes clung to its last rays flowing into infinity, then flickering and disappearing over the horizon. Night fell quickly, descended upon the man, and invaded his soul.

Some innate spark, instilled by the Creator, bound him to the ledge. His cognitive powers would send him plunging into the abyss; another force held him fast. Within him a desperate conflict raged. He sat and listened to the altercation within his soul as if he were only a disinterested onlooker.

The dank night air chilled his bones. He shivered. The heavy fog, typical in Kentucky's Appalachian Mountains, settled heavily upon him. He felt its weight constricting him. In slow motion, one by one, each protracted second ticked by. He peered into the ebony-thick wall of space.

He listened to the memory of Jenny's tears. Her jaw structure, shattered in the accident, precluded speech, yet he had understood her fully. For nine years they had held each other, caressed each other's hearts with understanding. How fragile those years, those moments, in retrospect, like a lily blooming, daily growing more wondrous—until the marauder called death stomped on the loveliness. Death was the enemy that struck in silent ambush. The lily was no more.

"Take care of Annie." With her eyes she'd pleaded. From between sterile hospital sheets, she'd given him her heart's message.

It was then he'd spoken his only lie to Jenny. "I'll take care of Annie. I'll love our daughter. Yes. I will always love our daughter."

Annie. Instantly killed when the drunk careening around the precarious Kentucky hills plowed into their small Honda. He'd take care of Annie. He would place flowers on her grave. Then he would crawl to Jenny's plot and beg to die.

The images lingered. He tortured himself with memory: her spontaneous, glorious laughter, her eyes sparkling with tender love, her hand caressing his cheek, her lips on his—forever to be—only a memory.

Jenny's face had relaxed. She squeezed his hand gently, softly, ever so softly, believing him, trusting him.

Then the light in her eyes had dimmed. The light—which had sparkled and laughed and bounced into his life, into his heart, into his soul—had died. The radiance of her laugh was gone. Her glittering, glowing spirit, which had warmed him and renewed him had departed.

As deep as this night's darkness, so also seemed the silence.

Little Annie. Delicate like a deep purple rose. With sunlight sparkling in her shiny hair, black and curly like his, her tiny dimples hiding playfully until the belly-laugh erupted, she'd tuck herself giggling in Daddy's arms, her long lashes demurely teasing. Since her first smile—or had the first merely been gas pains?—she had completely captivated him. Now, again just a part of earth's dust, she had returned to her source, his child with a broken neck.

He swayed, longing for the darkness to strangle him, to catapult him into the abyss. He despised the light that would bring a new day and the joy of new challenges to the oblivious world. There would be no joy in the life of a man who had thrown a rose on his wife's coffin and fallen to his knees, while the thud of dirt upon white pine boxes mocked the dignity of their lives.

As the requiem concluded, he had simply walked away, a stranger to humanity—a stranger among strangers who patted his shoulder kindly, but they would go home to sparkling fireplaces and the laughter of children dragging worn teddy bears while eating chocolate ice cream cones.

Two weeks ago upon this ledge, he and Jenny sat with Annie and admired the beauty of this new home, the Pine Mountain region of southeastern Kentucky, with its endless array of green hues, so antithetical to the red desert area of Arizona's central basin where they had been living. He'd clung to Annie, who at three, sniffed contemptuously at his acrophobia, her little heart wanting to peer over the edge. Far below, a country mountain road coiled itself, deceptive in its beauty, for it was preparing to strike with lethal accuracy.

This darkness was right! It should be dark! He sat upon a flat, cold rock and closed his eyes. Perhaps he slept. He wondered if years had passed or centuries or seconds.

When he opened his eyes, the world had changed. The shifting fog floated in silver shadows above him, gray ghosts straight from Hades, perhaps even waiting for Charon to ferry them across the rivers Acheron and Styx to the lower regions. Could he have somehow become a member of Dante's strange world of the living dead? Was he a walking corpse? The idea appealed to him.

In his dream-like trance, he noticed a tiny flickering light, like a firefly, in the valley below. Murky darkness spread over the whole of his world, yet the firefly riveted his attention. Could it be Ulysses, encased with Diomedes in Dante's punishing tongue of fire? Or was it a mere bug, something like himself, transient, fragile, whose essence could be squashed in a split second of incomprehensible pain?

The light zigged and zagged and diffused itself, revealing its narrow, meandering path. He leaned forward, curious. It moved through the interminable darkness around and up and closer to him. Might it be Cerebrus, the three-headed dog, which guarded the entrance to Hades to keep the living dead from entering the infernal region? Dante's *Inferno* didn't scare him.

The light appeared and disappeared and reappeared. It fascinated him. There was no sound, no crickets' song, no whizzing of bats' wings. No whispering leaves rustled in the night. There was only the tiny light below that now demanded the whole of his attention. He felt outside of himself, watching. He continued to monitor the movement of the light, as it grew brighter. It seemed to have a momentous purpose, like the sun, like the moon and stars that tucked themselves out of his reach this sorrowful night.

The light disappeared behind a ridge. He realized how desperate he was to have it return. He stretched out his hands and lurched forward, slipping on loose gravel, and cried into the disconsolate night. "O God, give to me the light."

Immediately as if in response, in the midst of an unearthly glow, not six feet from him, she stood. She was a young woman about Jenny's age, remarkably like Jenny in appearance, though somewhat indistinct in the radiating beam of the flashlight.

Ethereal in the fuzzy rolling mist, she regarded him with a gentle expression.

A halo-like cascade, her ash-blond hair just touched her tiny rounded shoulders. High cheekbones, deep blue eyes exuding kindness, a tiny upturned nose—she stirred him strangely. He felt as if he had entered into another life.

She spoke. Her resonant contralto voice attracted him. He longed to weep in her arms, not as a betrayal to Jenny, but for human comfort. He focused upon her words.

"I followed you here," she said simply. "Your grief stretches you beyond what you can endure alone." She moved to him and touched his arm, not provocatively but with an innocence born in another world.

The light in the flash she carried flickered. In the instant of darkness, she seemed to possess her own inward source of illumination. Somehow it seemed natural.

He sat in silence, watching her, listening to her.

"Jenny and Annie have not forgotten you. They are waiting where the light of love shines always."

The reminder aroused anger within him. Who was she to interfere with his sorrow? Yet he desperately wanted her to stay. He grasped her arm. Again she reached to him with her soothing words.

"I walked and talked with Jenny just last week. We met in the little chapel beyond the oak grove near the band shell."

He knew the place. Jenny spoke of it the day she'd taken Annie to the zoo. His desultory thoughts transported him again to Annie, her love of wild animals, especially the spotted, long-necked giraffe.

"If I climb the giraffe's neck, I'll reach to Heaven," she'd announced, and stretched her chubby arms to an imaginary celestial realm.

Jenny's eyes had held his as she responded to Annie's pronouncement. "No, Child. Only the Light of the World can get you there." Though she spoke to Annie, he knew the words were meant for him. Jenny's eyes had twinkled, the way they always did when she had some magnificent secret to share with him. But life's little exigencies had denied the opportunity for him to learn her thoughts. Then the accident.

He rested his head in his hands. "Life is a black hole," he declared. "I wish one would come tumbling out of space and fall on me."

Softly, she spoke again. "Light overcomes the darkness! The Light of This Sad World prepares a place for you, even now, with Jenny and Annie." She handed him her flashlight.

"Here! Read these words."

He focused the beam on the small black Book she held for him to read.

"I am the Light of the World," they proclaimed.

He contemplated the vastness of the black night suffocating him and the distant vestige of light that had illuminated his world. How his eyes had clung to that flickering glow! Suddenly, supernaturally, he grasped eternal truth: even a spark of light is stronger than the blackest darkness! For this epiphany, Jenny's words had prepared him.

Infinitesimal though it was, a tiny glimmer entered his spirit and caressed his sorrow. Understanding, acceptance, and unexpected purpose: gradually, imperceptibly—each began its embryonic journey into his soul.

"It's the man Jesus, isn't it. He's the answer. He can bring light, even to my darkness?

She nodded and smiled and gently placed the Book in his hands.

He leaned against a tree trunk and somehow absorbed its rugged strength. He closed his eyes and deeply inhaled fresh mountain air. A sudden outburst of rhapsodic tree frogs in a perfectly tuned chorus shattered the silence.

Trembling with unfamiliar emotion, he spoke softly. "Jenny, get our mansion ready, whatever that entails."

When his celestial visitor failed to respond to his words, he opened his eyes. He wanted her to know about the spark kindled in his heart, which would forever conquer the dark places. He desperately wanted her to know.

She had mystically, in complete silence, vanished into the inscrutable night. He sighed and dropped his head into his hands. He hadn't even heard her name.

The rolling vapors parted. He gazed up through the mist, catching this night's first glimpse of the moon's reflecting light. He clutched the Book against his heart and whispered, "Sweet Jenny, my little Annie, I've a mission here, for a while, a King to serve." He breathed deeply and deliberately.

On the saddest day of his life, in a strange place, with an unknown messenger, he had just made the most important and lasting commitment of his existence. Somehow he was aware that he was no longer alone.

He grasped the Book and considered its Light—the One who would guide him lovingly down the mountain, and someday, into a golden mansion where a woman with flowing ash-blond hair gloriously laughed, and where a little girl with black, curly hair danced happily within transparent, light-filled walls.

He turned and began the descent into a sin-darkened world.

He held in his heart the Light for which it was desperate.

For God, who commanded the light to shine out of
darkness,
hath shined in our hearts,
to give the light of the knowledge of the glory of God
in the face of Jesus Christ.
We are troubled on every side, yet not distressed;
we are perplexed, but not in despair
while we look not at the things which are seen, but at
the things which are not seen.
for the things which are seen are temporal;
but the things which are not seen are eternal.

II Corinthians 4:6, 8, 18

To Denise—sister. You bring light WHEREVER you go.
You are an angel of light in my life.

And

To Myrtle—our mother—our sweet, laughing light.

A Message on the Wind

Whatsoever the Lord pleased,
that did he in heaven,
and in earth, in the seas, and all deep places.
He causeth the vapours to ascend from the ends of the earth;
He maketh lightnings for the rain;
He bringeth the wind out of his treasuries.

Psalm 135:6, 7

Again, the impish wind snatched a stray curl and playfully tickled her cheek. Hot white sand trickled through her fingers, a few tenacious granules clinging. Impatiently turning her sleek, young form under the ruthless eye of the garish sun, she provocatively nudged him with the tip of a well- manicured toenail.

The fickle breeze had lingered for a while, tantalizing her with invisible caresses; unkindly it withdrew to chase a small child's homemade kite. Bronze had deepened into dangerous red. The penetrating warmth for which she'd cajoled him so enticingly had offered little satisfaction. She'd been impatient to come. Now she wanted to go.

Gently he questioned, "Why are you so restless—like the capricious wind?"

She could offer no answer.

The air conditioned, velvet-cushioned Mercedes embraced her weariness. Canada Dry on crushed ice trickled away the dry, parched ache of her throat. While strains of Mendelssohn's Concerto in E Minor soothed her impatience, she contemplated an intellectual romp into the philosophies of the Indian *Upanishads*, definitely stimulating—temporarily at least. And of course, he—would be a pleasant diversion.

Tall, muscular, sun-darkened, rugged—this blond Apollo did possess fleeting appeal. His blue eyes, looking intently at her, sparkled intelligence and friendliness. He chuckled deep in his throat, easily and often. She yearned to love him, to be one in spirit with him, but somehow she knew he would be like the others. The graveyard of her broken romances stretched across the windblown island that was her kingdom.

The motor whirred softly, unheard and unappreciated. She took little notice of the plush luxury of her world as the Mercedes hurtled past exotic, rare orchids framed in Maidenhair ferns and Sphagnum moss. Once, the lush, deep green gardens had intrigued the talent of her imagination. Now the car and its occupants whizzed uncaring through paradise, climbing steadily and easily to her summit penthouse. Like the Greek god at her side and his predecessors, already more or less a memory, one orchard merged into another.

From atop the mountain, they paused to view the never-questioning river, cascading faithfully to its briny destiny. Every morning misty vapors rose sleepily to mate with indiscriminate, unsolicited lovers, sending forth offspring to freshen the earth. It would all happen again and there would be no regrets. *Like myself,* she reflected. Fleetingly, she pondered if she, indeed, could ever admit to regrets, past or present.

I suppose, she conceded silently, *there's a time for just about everything under the sun.*

Suddenly weary, she craved solitude.

Reluctant, he hesitated; then he drove away. She didn't watch him leave.

She regarded the orange ball of light trudging its evening patrol over the horizon and wondered what she'd do tomorrow. "Catch the elusive wind?" She laughed without humor. She'd tried that before.

To the west, high above the brilliant golden pathway of the departing sun, a tropical evening storm was fast developing. Oppressive black clouds whirled like frenzied dancers without a choreographer. Mesmerized, she watched the chaos in the heavens. "Undirected, like my existence," she admitted to the clap of thunder that bolted her into movement.

She sighed and headed into her alpine villa, completely indifferent to its extravagant charms, which in the past had been the focus of her aspirations.

Rich cedar walls imported from Lebanon whispered their fragrance into every room. An acre of tinted glass windows, draped in Phoenician purple linen, afforded an unobstructed mountain view of creation's grandeur, splendor from every direction. An original Van Gogh, a playground of blue, green, and gray hues, reflected the opulent taste of the designer-occupant. Reposing on a nest of ornately-carved tables from Hong Kong, an ancient Roman sculpture—impassive and solemn—stared interminably at nothing. From his frozen lips, he issued forth no wisdom.

Exotic melodic strains of oriental flutes wailed their melancholy from camouflaged speakers embedded in gigantic clusters of tropical ferns. Rare somber parrots, adorned in iridescence, squawked incessantly, stupidly; a former suitor had taught them to proclaim, "Vanity, vanity, life's vanity." Once-valued busts of Plato and Aristotle lay haplessly discarded, one tucked between cushions, the other dropped carelessly upon plush nylon pile.

She sat alone in the twilight, the storm now raging full force upon the mountain. The parrots croaked at the tropical fish insanely racing in endless orbits. She turned her attention to the spectacle whirling in from the west. She watched lightning torment the clouds like a matador flipping an electric cape at an enraged bull, the roar of the victim rumbling and echoing among the thrilled onlookers.

The tempest unleashed itself and doggedly pursued the zig-zagging cape in torrential fury. Seeking escape, the ponderous clouds hurled themselves through nothingness, crashing and merging and roaring until her mountain summit shook with the vibrations of battle. Wide-eyed and insignificant, she sat spellbound, peering through rain-spattered glass.

A crash startled her into activity. She grimaced, realizing the impotence of man. The wind's power had made simple work of intruding into her library. Easy prey, electricity had gone dead, victim of the storm's fury. She stumbled through the dark to the room in which the wisdom of philosophy had systematically and obstinately denied her answers.

She slammed the shutter and locked it. Tripping over a small pile of forgotten volumes, which obviously had toppled in the whirlwind, she bent, appropriated the closest, and prepared to pass another sleepless night in futility.

For just a moment she longed for Apollo, but she knew his presence would be inconsequential. The loneliness nagged at her from within just as did the constant storm of questions.

She knew by experience that life's most significant moments—pain, death, confrontation with truth—had to be faced alone.

She pawed through a desk drawer and pulled out a candle and a box of old matches. Through the hushed darkness with the book clutched to her bosom, she felt her way back to the east window.

She paused and watched the swirling tempest in the sky. "Out there, it's exactly like my soul," she confessed aloud to the silence. The silence would offer no comfort. It would not answer her.

Lighting the wick, she watched the flame flicker and then burn strong and steady. With the tiny radiance her only guide, she opened the fragile pages of the black leather volume and withdrew herself from the frenzy which rumbled around her mountain. The candle flickered, but burned on, encouraging.

As the minutes plodded dutifully through eternity and the planet sped relentlessly toward infinity, for her, time and movement ceased.

For out of the stormy darkness that had been her existence, from the pages of a randomly-selected Book, softly there walked a Man wearing dusty sandals.

He stood upon the waters and the waves curled in obeisance, rolling over and over like adoring puppies wanting their bellies scratched.

He stood upon the mountain and uttered a life-philosophy that tumbled down and reverberated into stormy hearts, and mighty men dropped to their knees.

To the objects of His eternal affection, He affirmed with His life and with His words, "I am the Way, the Truth, the Life." To every storm that would torment these objects of His eternal affection, He commanded, "Peace, be still."

He hung, bloody and broken, while lightning lashed dismay at the folly of men, and the birds secluded under their own wings trembled, and the very stones on the rain-soaked ground shook in terror.

The candle glowed stronger. The wind slammed itself against her transparent refuge in a suicidal attempt to whiff out the light. Even the mighty wind would never extinguish the answer that had begun to radiate within her. The storm surrendered and moved on.

She closed the book and like the mighty men, knelt, that she might reach up above the storm, above the sun, above the searching eyes of men—reach right into the heart of the One who had conquered all storms.

In the eastern sky, from whence He would one day appear, a smiling crescent moon tiptoed, scattering reflected glory. She thought of Apollo. Perhaps—he'd like the name Matthew better—or Bartholemew.

She laughed with pure joy. She had captured God's message on the wind.

> *Vanity of vanities,*
> *saith the Preacher, vanity of vanities;*
> *all is vanity.*
> *What profit hath a man of all his labor which he taketh*
> *under the sun?*
> *I made me great works;*
> *I builded me house; I planted me vineyards:*
> *I made me gardens and orchards,*
> *and I planted trees in them of all kinds of fruits:*
> *I gathered me also silver and gold,*
> *and the peculiar treasure of kings and of the provinces:*
> *and whatsovever mine eyes desired I kept not from them,*
> *then I looked on all the works that my hands had wrought,*
> *and, behold, all was vanity and vexation of spirit, and*
> *there was no profit*
> *under the sun.*

Ecclesiastes 1:2,3; 2: 4-11

Let us hear the conclusion of the whole matter:
fear God, and keep his commandments:
for this is the whole duty of man.

Ecclesiastes 12:13

Dedicated to Greg—nephew. Like Solomon, you have
been given the gift of intellect;
Praise God, for in mind, emotion, will – in totality,
you have grasped and cherished God's message on the wind.

The Carpenter's Son

*He maketh the barren woman to keep house,
and to be a joyful mother of children.*

Psalm 113:9

Joe had fashioned the little cottage out of oak logs next to a crystalline mountain lake. Its walls had welcomed them eagerly after a short honeymoon trip camping in the Colorado Mountains. It had inhaled the aroma of freshly baked brown bread, spice cake, and pot roast over young carrots. It had reveled in the thrill of young laughter and whispered secrets.

That was in the past.

Now, shattered dreams lingered menacingly in its corners. In the tenth year of this marriage, silence brooded, roamed through all the rooms of the little cottage hewn in love out of oak logs.

Silence permeated the tiny bedroom at the other end of the hall. Never occupied, its loneliness cried out for fulfillment. Often they stood in the room where a small blue-and-white checkered blanket draped the empty cradle that he had carved from the creativity of his love. Royal blue curtains hung limp in the sterility of the closed room. A black-eyed teddy bear sat obediently where the excited couple had placed it eight years ago. Its sorrowful, beady eyes focused on the unused crib. A motley clown lamp rested next to a pile of newborn diapers, which had yellowed during years of neglect.

"I can't do it. I can't. I can't face it." Elise sought his eyes for comfort.

"Send a card with regrets and a gift." He whispered into her hair, avoiding the despair in her hollow eyes. "Someday we'll have our own child. Then you'll want to welcome others. Tonight, just stay here with me."

He'd watched the sparkle in her eyes grow dim, the lilt in her laugh dissipate. Even her hair had changed color, darkened a shade or two from her sorrow. Several miscarriages and three tubal pregnancies had nearly stolen her from him. At the least, they'd absconded with her joy.

Elise cried in his arms. "Women were meant to be mothers. I am a barren woman. I have no purpose."

"Your purpose is to love me," Joe pleaded.

"I do, oh, I do."

He understood. Her soul seemed these days encased in gloom and self-reproach. Was there no comfort for her distress?

The inevitable lay ahead—the battery of routine medical tests, expensive, often embarrassing, probably futile. The next day he dialed a fertility specialist.

Months of testing, pain . . . HOPE, side effects . . . HOPE, mounting costs . . . CRUSHED HOPE. Well-meaning acquaintances frequently inquired, "Oh, why haven't you had any children? Don't you want to have children?"

They clung to each other. The rollercoaster ride of emotion left them breathless and more than a little bruised.

Month after month, in anxious expectancy, they stood gazing in the doorway of the little blue room and dreamed of a hungry wail in the night, the cooing sound of a contented infant eagerly accepting warm milk, brown eyes, and a searching little hand patting his mama's face.

The young husband spent long evening hours sculpturing a perfect oak rocking chair that wouldn't creak. She watched and smiled.

Then the rollercoaster came to a desperate, shrieking halt, a monster roaring in finality, as it hurled them from the track with a single word from the specialist, "Hopeless!"

Throats tight with swallowed sorrow, they stumbled home and without speaking closed the door to the nursery. The little bear sat alone and stared at the empty crib.

He held her close, though he knew that human comfort would not rescue her from the black hole of despair into which that up-and-down ride had deposited her. Even the love she'd committed to him dwelled in her head only; her heart had toppled from the rollercoaster directly into the pit and shattered beyond repair. Of that he was convinced.

Elise continued the perfunctory routine of her existence. She scrubbed immaculate walls, swept the sparkling floor, rearranged orderly closets. She did not enter the little blue room at the end of the hall.

He brought her a small dog, a wiggly, brown-eyed poodle with a friendly tail.

"It's a baby I want. She ran to her bed and flung herself into its mute comfort. Her goose-down pillow was wet.

"We'll adopt," he suggested, searching desperately for solace to ease her heartache, some respite to distract their sorrow.

"No! I want my own child." She began to weep again.

Years of shared frustration had drawn them close. Now the young husband, barely thirty, looked at his beloved with total helplessness. Sighing, he left the room and walked out into the night.

He sat upon a fallen log by the mountain lake. The moon glowed, its reflection mute upon the quiet water. The treetops, their dark shadows restless in the breeze, swayed above the murky dampness of the evening. Across the lake the skyline was dim, nearly indiscernible. Heat lightning splayed its flares in ever-widening declarations of splendor. Stars twinkled, their little lights mirrored in the rippling lake shadows.

Across the water, a colicky newborn wailed. The crickets ceased their concert to listen.

He dropped his head in his hands and wept, for her, for himself, for the child they could never have. Though it seemed ludicrous to him, he cried even for the little dog, rejected by a gentle but broken woman who had always loved dogs, especially apricot toy poodles.

He felt himself also slipping into the black pit of despondency. An indistinct silhouette in the moonlight—he stood up, clenched both fists, and pummeled an invisible enemy. "Why, God?" He leaned against the innocent tree he had struck.

He raised one fist and shook it at Heaven. "God!" Agitated and desperate, he choked on his rising voice.

A whiff of breeze, like a cool, soft hand ruffled his hair. A low rumble of omnipotence growled benevolently from the edge of the horizon. The moon smiled at him as it lingered between drifting clouds. A fish jumped and splashed into the opaque water. Everywhere he turned, his senses touched mystery, movement, beauty, and wondrous life. In the calmness of the quiet night, he heard a still, small voice and comprehended its message. With his soul and with his spirit, he embraced that message fully.

"God." The word had wondrously transformed into a prayer.

Like a flash of lightning, the answer was illuminated from within his memory, fragmented at first, yet profound and powerful in glorious possibility. "In the fullness of time, God sent forth his son . . . to redeem . . . that we might receive the adoption of sons . . ."

Adoption.

It was the answer for him, now, in this moment. It would be the answer for them.

Remembering his grandfather's Bible and loving admonitions, Joe repeated aloud that long-forgotten promise—almost inaudibly at first to the moon-ripples, then to the reflection of the stars, even to the love-sick crickets, and finally, confidently, to the growling rumble at the horizon. Hearing himself repeat the words—*the adoption of sons*—made it real, made it right.

He would go to her and talk to her and she would know it was right, that it had come from the heart and will of God. Deep within his awareness, he had known the solution, and so had she. They had simply tucked it away, out of reach, and covered it over with their sorrow.

Suddenly, Elise was there by his side, her hand grasping his in the moonlight. The still, small voice had spoken also to her.

Together they knelt.

Lightning crowned the horizon with radiance. A horned owl winked at them in its blaze. In the fragrance of a pine-scented cathedral, they clung to each other, sharing tears of renewal as they bathed in the comforting refreshment of agape love.

Together they ascended out of the pit.

A cricket symphony accompanied them back to the little cottage hewn in love out of oak logs. Completing the celebration, a flurry of lightning bugs, fireflies rarely seen in Colorado, lit their pathway home with unexpected grandeur, their flamboyant, tiny lanterns glimmering all the way. Laughter erupted as Joe and Elise harmonized with the crickets and playfully chased the elusive lights.

*

They awoke early. Munching on hot, buttered cinnamon rolls, they watched a blue jay tease a whippoorwill in the bird feeder. A fluffy-tailed brown squirrel below the feeder scampered in circles, gobbling the remains of seeds. Four fleet, funny, frolicsome squirrel siblings appeared from nowhere; a nimble game of tag ensued. The young couple howled in shared delight.

Always the opportunist, the little dog, finally sensing his welcome, joyfully eased his way up into his mistress's lap and rolled over for a delicious belly-scratch and perhaps a small bite of buttered bread.

They walked to the room at the other end of the hall and opened the door. Elise leaned, trembling against Joe's shoulder. It was time to go.

*

Black letters on the heavy, age-stained door affronted them. The word ADOPTIONS whispered hope. At the same time it shouted fear.

Suzanne met them with a solemn face. "We've many couples. Few babies." Her prognosis was guarded, even grim.

"Put us on your list," Joe said without hesitation.

"It could be months, or years," she told them. "You must be prepared."

"The Carpenter's Son is in control," he said confidently. "Before the world existed, He knew the child who would be ours." He leaned over to confirm the correct spelling of his name.

Suzanne smiled. She, too, had discovered strength in the Carpenter's Son.

They climbed on the rollercoaster again, this time cushioned in the gentleness of His love. Still the ride was not easy. Visits, interviews, uncertainty, intimate questions. With every jangle of their phone, a tremor of excited terror smothered their breaths.

The days grew short. Winter's grayness and bluster sought to strangle hope, but the door to the little room at the other end of the hall remained open. The little dog grew fat on remnants of brown bread, spice cake, and pot roast over carrots.

Finally, blossoms adorned apple trees in soft pink. Green buds and then glowing red fruit appeared; the bounty turned into steaming summer pies. Fish jumped happily in the lake, gulping delectable dragonflies. Heat lightning often dazzled the evening skyline, while crickets serenaded the pensive-looking owl.

Leaves, yellow and orange, floated lazily to the earth. A fat pumpkin with a toothless grin leered mischievously at them. Little wax Pilgrims stood tall upon their table of hospitality while the small child who lived across the lake toddled around their home chasing the little dog and dragging the black-eyed teddy bear.

Snow curtained the landscape with intricate lace. Ice settled upon the lake, holding tight the ripples. "It's time to get a tree," Joe said. They trudged on webbed snowshoes around the lake. Her favorite tree, a small blue spruce, willingly offered them its beauty. Soon they sat cross-legged before the fireplace stringing white bursts of popcorn, reminiscing, laughing, dreaming, planning.

Suddenly the little dog leaped, yipping in an outburst of concerned emotion.

Suzanne, with snow-wet eyelashes, entered quickly, protecting a tiny bundle wrapped in blue. "I by-passed a few little procedures—it's okay—you are now parents. He's only seven days old." She lifted the protection of the woolen blanket.

They stood paralyzed with astonishment.

"Well, I can bring him back to the Home for Christmas, if you've changed your minds." She laughed, enjoying their ecstasy.

Years of heartache vanished in that moment as two dark brown eyes squinted up in his first glimpse of his father and mother. He yawned. "Look," Elise murmured. "He smiled at me."

Suzanne deposited a gift-wrapped package. "Enough stuff in here for a couple of days. Come on in and see me on Monday. Merry Christmas!" She vanished into white darkness.

The young mother sat holding a warm bottle, listening to contented sounds of her son taking nourishment. His little fingers opened and closed upon her cheeks. His legs moved and stretched in the blue-checkered flannel. Through her tears she whispered the purpose of their existence. "I can't wait to tell you about God." She sang softly of Mary's Little Lamb. The fat apricot poodle, curled upon his mistress's slippers, slept.

The young carpenter pulled a chair close, kissed his wife's hair, watched the joy sparkle in her eyes, stared in wonder at the miracle clutching his thumb. He thought of another man named Joseph gazing the first time at a tiny baby clinging to His stepfather's thumb. He wondered aloud, "Did Joseph realize those little hands would be the focus of man's redemption and of his praise—throughout eternity?" He watched the peaceful infant. "I want you to meet the Carpenter's Son," he affirmed. The fire crackled contentedly in the hearth.

Somewhere far away and long ago, an angel had proclaimed a message—the most important message mankind would ever hear—"UNTO US A SON IS GIVEN."

The little cottage in the woods and its inhabitants totally understood the impact of that message.

> *But when the fullness of the time was come,*
> *God sent forth his Son,*
> *made of a woman,*
> *made under the law*
> *to redeem them that were under the law,*
> *that we might receive the adoption of sons*
> *and because ye are sons*
> *God hath sent forth the Spirit of his Son into your hearts,*
> *Crying Abba, Father.*

Wherefore thou art no more a servant, but a son
and if a son then an heir of God through Christ.

Galatians 4:4-7

Dedicated to Joy—daughter-in-law.
You also are mother extraordinare.
Mother of my grandsons—Aiden and Peyton.
I'm so thankful you love and honor the Carpenter's Son.

The Rock That Stood Firm

The Lord is my rock,
and my fortress, and my deliverer;
In whom I will trust;
my buckler, and the horn of my salvation,
and my high tower.
I will call upon the Lord,
who is worthy to be praised . . .
In my distress I called upon the Lord,
and cried unto my God:
then the earth shook and trembled;
the foundations also of the hills moved and were
shaken. . .
because he was wroth.

Psalm 18:2-4, 6, 7

Matt wiped his brow with a mud-streaked forearm. Fresh blood oozed from scrapes on his fingers and smudged his gray-tweed suit coat and trousers. He felt no pain for the moment; surprisingly, he felt no terror, only gripping fatigue. The astonishing events of the past few hours had numbed him.

With the wonder of modern technology, he was watching it happen. Strapped to his wrist, a miniature transistorized television featured grimfaced reporters unable to mask their frantic despair. The world, they announced, was literally crumbling, disintegrating, bit by bit.

It had started only a few days before when a bloody conflagration had erupted at a China-Russia border crossing. Both Moscow and Peking and miles of surrounding land simply floated away like finely-ground dust inhaled by a whirlwind. In response, the stock market plummeted. Everywhere on the planet, men's hearts failed from fear.

The Florida Keys slowly broke into pieces and sank. Huge condominiums toppled into the swirling depths. Bald eagles screamed in confusion as they lifted from their high nests, built on utility poles along US I. Instinctively, they winged northward.

The rumbling of another and another earth-splitting cataclysm moved in waves from the west. The Rockies crumbled, flinging into space large boulders, meteors as cold and hard as men's hearts. The Earth was shuddering in its orbit.

Matt looked up at the sparkling, gigantic rock, before which he stood, its towering whiteness blazoning its invitation. This mammoth refuge had miraculously ascended, displacing the golden wheat fields of Arkansas, Kansas, and Missouri. Its origin was undetermined. Perhaps it had always been there, hovering just below the earth's crust, waiting, always ready to provide for man's deepest need, but until this catastrophic day, unnoticed, ignored, even cast aside.

Scaling the albescence presented a task more onerous than he'd ever tackled during all his years of self-sufficiency and success. His efforts to claw his way to the top had only bloodied his fingers and his clothes in the process and left him panting with the exertion. He had no clue for solving this most prodigious enigma.

Next to him, a young couple, stocked with pitons, ropes, karabiners—all the latest and best in spikes and links for climbing—dumped their shiny new gear in a heap.

"The screws won't hold," the bedraggled young wife beseeched her husband. Her puffy eyes filled with tears; dark shadows emphasized her strain.

"The wall is too slick. It can't be climbed. All my experience is useless." He sank to the ground. The infant, sensing her parents' despair, squawked and squirmed in the backpack.

With the dismayed young couple, Matt stepped back and looked up, squinting in the brightness. Crowned with cumulus light-filled clouds, the top of the great rock was obscured. As Earth's travail momentarily subsided, they listened to a hauntingly beautiful melody, which floated down and rested upon them. Something exceedingly wonderful was available at the top of this rock.

"I comprehend but a little," said the young man, whose daughter had finally succumbed to her need for sleep. "The rock of my salvation . . . that's all I hear . . . whatever that means."

The young mother wept in her husband's arms. "It doesn't get us safely to the top." They shuffled away, hopeless, with heads lowered.

The Earth's groaning continued beneath him. He eyed the rock—strong, immobile, firm.

A watch-sized television announcer related a drought in Argentina, a tidal wave surging over the Philippines, the disappearance of Greenland . . .

A few feet from him, a leather-jacketed youth with wavy, dark hair roared toward the white rock on a monstrous Harley-Davidson cycle. Surely he couldn't reach the top with such a foolish stunt. With engines fully revved, he accelerated and approached at top speed. Amazingly, he climbed—for a few suspended seconds—then toppled to the base where he lay atop the pile of twisted, useless metal. He got up, kicked the junk heap with a spiked boot and stomped away, raging.

All around Matt, the multitudes, seeking rescue, moved in and squatted at the base of the rock, many weeping and gnashing teeth. All were like him, alone, exhausted, despondent. Men dressed in rags, ripped and bloodied by the wars and constant battles of life, sat as mere shadows of despair, longing for a glimmer of hope.

Matt listened to the broadcaster's drone.

Inflation soars to 500%. One half of the world's population is said to have AIDS. The divorce rate is up to one in one. Another gigantic chemical spill in Saskatchawan. Great Britain is no longer a part of this earth. Kids popping LSD smile as they float into space, never cognizant of when the last breath is taken. New Zealand, also reported as a casualty.

High above the rock, a Blue Angel squadron sizzled through the sky and spewed a human cargo of parachutists. The giant mechanical birds, then set on automatic pilot, shrilled over the land to the Atlantic and dove to a green-foamed graveyard.

In anger and jealousy, the multitudes at the base of the rock stood screaming curses at those, who by their profession, had been able to float down to safety. Within minutes, however, a cloud of puffy chutes mushroomed into sight. All of the fliers landed upon the earth at the base of the rock.

"From up there, we can't even see the top," an earth-bound pilot cried to his terrified audience."

"Must be the sun's glare," suggested a pragmatic officer, who in disgust was ripping away useless muslin.

Matt contemplated the failure of the military pilots. A different judicious approach to the top might prove more effective. With his hand patting the fat wad of bills he'd snatched on the way out of his New York apartment, he made his way through the despairing crowds, all gazing at the rock, all longing to unfold its mysteries. Down into the valley he hobbled on blistered feet until he came to his destination. Others had already formed lines at the county's helicopter rescue service.

Many were turned away for lack of funds. He took heart. Fumbling in his pocket for bills, he waited, listening to the fire-water sizzling below the thin, precarious crust called land. Finally he scurried toward the little machine, ducking to avoid being gashed by the whirling relentlessness of the blades. UP they soared. The glistening whiteness loomed majestically before them. As they climbed, the top seemed ever to beckon, but they could not attain it. Finally a gentle cyclone blew them circling away and down. Try as they might, they could not approach the summit. With sorrowful eyes, the pilot responded apologetically to Matt's queries.

"We keep trying. We keep hoping we can make it. I must drop you off away from the others. Hope you understand, Buddy."

The copter left him somewhere in Iowa. Like the souls of men, the land was gray and dismal. The corn, once abundant in promise, drooped, for nature also recognized and responded to the crumbling lives of humans.

In the midst of all the despair, one glimmer of hope continued to impress Matt's thoughts. Here and there, somehow possessing the security of the mountain experience, there would appear a man dressed in clean linen. He would stride confidently, safely, never stepping on land where the earth was weak. Though sometimes attacked, he would cling to the black leather Book, which these Mountain Men all treasured, and would emerge from the affliction unscathed.

"Don't slip into the abyss," one of them cried to a beautiful, raven-eyed Chinese girl. "Look in this Book," he begged, "and learn the only way to the top of the mountain."

"Too easy," she rasped. "I know there is more to it than that." She trudged away in tears, wringing her hands.

"No fun!" yowled another as he defiantly raised the decibel level on his ghetto buster and suddenly exploded into a whirl-wind. For a split second, his eyes were wide with surprise. Then he was gone.

"I want to get there on my own," screamed another in arro-gance. He scooped up a handful of mud and flicked it at the man in white. He jumped on a small Honda, gunned it, rode off, and sank into a hole of hot lava. The mud turned to fine dust and whirled away in tiny eddies.

The man in white sank to his knees, clutching his Book, and cried. The wind wailed. The lava gurgled under their feet. It was unnerving. The world continued to tremble in throes of destruction.

Matt watched the Mountain Men. He heard their song, the same melody that had wafted its haunting sweetness upon his senses while he'd trembled at the bottom of the white rock. He recognized that the great secret—the route to the safety of the rock—was written in the Book which they carried.

The world's misfortunes continued to create havoc. A war of brother against brother. New York City gone like the explosion of a Molotov cocktail. All men reported to be laboring fervently, yet fruitlessly, to attain the security available only on the white mountain.

Finally, Matt began an earnest search for a Mountain Man in white linen, possessing the Book.

He stumbled into a clearing. There, a man fifty yards from him pleaded earnestly with a group of epicureans, who were swaggering off, laughing in ill-fated levity. "Eat, drink, by all means be merry," they roared in hysterics. "For tomorrow we die!" A high tenor voice sang the final refrain off key in falsetto.

"They wouldn't even consider . . ." the man in white proclaimed resonantly to the sky.

The voice startled him. "Luke?" It was, indeed, his own brother.

The ground beneath Matt was shaking dangerously. "Throw me the Book," Matt shouted. "I am desperate for the Book!"

Instantly, his brother tossed it, just as he had sailed endless rubber footballs in their backyard on Long Island a millennium ago.

Matt opened the Book. Etched upon white pages, the image of a Man stretched upon a tree held him motionless. Distorted by incredible agony, the face still gazed at him with penetrating compassion. "I AM THE ROCK." The words leaped off the page and into his heart.

The tiny, floating island upon which Matt clung was crumbling. He dropped to one knee. The outer crust was melting away, disintegrating. From somewhere the flash of a nuclear explosion puffed fire into the sky.

He collapsed and lay prone on his tiny chunk of earth, which heaved and dipped with the movement of the waves. His face begrimed with the dust of the earth, he cried out, "Jesus Christ is the rock of my salvation."

Even as he clung desperately to a few slippery clumps of grass, instant peace descended. Should he die in the swirling volcano of Earth's last groan, Christ would be there. If he found himself shriveled and decayed at the bottom of the sea, the great God Jesus would be there.

"For me to live is Christ, to die is gain." Where had the words come from? He only knew they were words of eternal truth.

Then he realized he was no longer reeling on a tiny piece of Earth's dirt. His hands moving apprehensively upon his tweed suit revealed it was no longer ripped or grimy or stained with blood. In fact, it was no longer tweed; it was white linen. He leaped up in astonishment. His fatigue had vanished.

There watching him, grinning broadly, sat his brother Luke, cradling another Book. All around him delicate mountain flowers arrayed in rainbows of color swayed and bowed in deference to the cool breeze, also characteristic of a high place. A sprawling lion lounging in a bed of violets rumbled a friendly growl as a playful lamb bounded from behind a myrtle bush and landed on the lion's neck. Could it be it the wind, or were the flowers themselves singing the song of eternal love flowing both into and from Matt's heart? Matt could not detect the source of the music. Perhaps the celestial music originated in his very own soul; he knew only that it thrilled him.

Matt walked to the edge of the rock and gazed down at the world hating itself into oblivion. He beckoned his brother.

"Are you ready to go?" Luke asked. "Now that you are a true Mountain Man?"

Matt nodded, hefted a supply of life-filled Books, and easily followed Luke down the precipitous cliff. The man now dressed in fine linen was singing.

And a man shall be as an hiding place form the wind,
and a covert from the tempest
as rivers of water in a dry place,
as the shadow of a great rock in a weary land.

Isaiah 32:2

Dedicated to Paul—husband. For your firm footing on
the Rock,
I have a lifetime of gratitude.

Armed and Ready to Soar

He shall cover thee with his feathers,
and under his wings shalt thou trust:
his truth shall be thy shield and buckler.
Thou shalt not be afraid for the terror by night;
nor for the arrow that flieth by day . . .

Psalm 91:4, 5

A shadowy cloud floated ominously across the half-circle of the moon. Out of the mist, a ball of flame sizzled white and fell disintegrating a blackberry bush a few feet from them.

Lisa stifled a scream. She must not alert the enemy to their position. She clutched at David's sleeve, ripping faded cotton. He encircled her with muscular arms and pulled her face close into his chest. She sobbed silently.

"They're getting too close. We must keep going." David's voice, tender with a new husband's love, urged her on as he grasped her arms and guided her stumbling through the brush, over fallen trees, into the dark yawning throat of night.

Less than a mile away a battery of gun fire tick-a-ticked through the fog. A wild animal howled in death throes. Or was it one of them?

"Hurry," he pleaded urgently as she hesitated, listening.

Fatigue gripped her muscles. Strands of limp, jet-black hair clung to salty wetness and dried upon her cheeks.

Almost, she could not remember how many days they had been behind enemy lines, fleeing the relentless onslaught. They had recorded the enemy's strategies. A detailed report would be given when they returned to camp—if they returned.

She stumbled on a protruding rock and lurched to her right knee. She groaned in pain. Her breath came in arduous gasps. The ache behind her temples widened and deepened and she became aware of her throbbing pulse.

"We'll rest a moment," David conceded. "I'm exhausted also." From a muddy, tattered backpack, he pulled a small woolen blanket, laid it on the ground, and helped Lisa maneuver herself into a resting position. As they leaned against a large maple and listened to the moaning of the wind, the moon emerged from behind a cloud, eerie, iridescent in the fog. She rubbed her throbbing knee and eased herself against his chest.

"I shouldn't have let you come," he said.

"Nobody can escape this battle," she replied. "I'd rather be here with you."

She closed her eyes. Comforted by his warmth, she fell into a fitful sleep. The mist wandered aimlessly, companion to the silent darkness that blanketed the jaded pair.

The soft sound of swooping bats fluttered in the trees. A bobwhite whistled for his mate. The cold hardness of the earth penetrated her senses; in his arms she stiffened into awareness.

She stood and stretched, trying to ignore intense hunger. She pulled her jacket strings tighter against the chill of early morning. They moved again into the fog.

Somewhere along the way they had lost their automatic weapons. Though impotent against the gathered forces pursing them, the guns had offered a few moments of illusory comfort. Now the young warriors felt helpless. Enemy guerrillas could be anywhere. Furtively, they moved on, exhausted, vulnerable.

In the first of morning's attacks, a ruthless cannon belched venom. Concurring, a tank roared, evil in its intent. Bits of shrapnel from an exploding fireball sailed confidently over them and fell, singing a shrill dirge. They covered their heads with their arms and dove to the mud. Filth streaked their faces and their ripped clothing.

Dark shadows encircled her sunken, glazed eyes. Mud caked in her once-silky hair.

He looked at her intently. "You look terrible," he laughed, "but, oh, how I do love you."

With her hands she caressed the week's stubble irritating his cheeks. She smiled. For a lovely human moment the enemy threat vanished, but only for a moment.

Refreshed a little from their short rest, they trekked again through the dangerous back yard of their foe into the dawn of the sixth day.

They were desperate for weapons, new and strong, first to forestall and then to triumph. Theirs was not an enemy, however, to be conquered with conventional arms. His war plan included deceit and hedonism, faithlessness and despair, intimidation and utter destruction. His web of snares had been cleverly designed to entrap, to weaken, and finally to devour.

Above them a white-tailed, bald eagle, supreme ruler of the sky, plunged like a meteor. Fascinated, they stopped to watch. With a cry of victory, it plummeted toward a fish hawk, cruising imperiously on an airshaft, clutching its prey. Startled, the hawk released its catch in midair. With a swoop the eagle held the hawk's meal in his talons; then strangely, it gently released the victim, which plunged, thrashing its desperate fins all the way down into the safety of the cold alpine lake below. The majestic king of the sky spread its seven-foot wingspan and drifted easily to land atop a tall pine. The vanquished hawk fluttered away in frustrated defeat.

David and Lisa longed for strength to rise up in power as the eagle.

Hand in hand they ran through the underbrush, panting. The chilly, fresh mountain air burned their lungs with fire. Fear charred their souls. They sensed rather than saw the enemy's nearness. Headlong into the densest part of the forest they scrambled.

Suddenly they were struggling in a web, woven by their own despair and lack of faith. Before them, arrayed in black silk, stood the supreme commander of the enemy forces. He was smiling benignly and sniffing into a black silk kerchief. Gaudy sequins covered his attire. Awesome in power, he towered over the trembling young captives clinging to each other on the ground.

As the commander spoke, his left eye, only his left eye, frequently shifted. During that moment—convulsed by a strange struggle of power, as if a grievous flaw in his essence revealed itself—an indescribable malevolence clouded his countenance. He summoned his lieutenant general.

"Our guests are gaunt from their long, foolish run." His voice sounded like a mixture of granulated honey and thick maple syrup. He bowed stiffly, his plastic smile unchanging. His teeth were yellow. "Prepare them refreshment."

The lieutenant general led them into a forest-green army van, obviously designed to camouflage. Before them lay a lavish spread. Every kind of fresh fruit, dripping with moisture; golden puffs of aromatic breads, soaked with newly churned country butter; filet mignon sizzling in its own juices; baby vegetables—peas and fat cobs of butter-drenched salted corn.

The tall commander motioned to them. "Enjoy. This is the reason for living." Gallantly, he held a velvet-cushioned chair for her.

Nearly famished, they eyed the table of their enemy, an enemy whose war plans had burned into their memory. They'd heard him address his troops.

The noon sun high above cast flickering shadows of warning.

Lightning flared in the clear blue sky—another warning? The bald eagle sat, watching from his perch atop the tall pine tree.

David spoke without hesitation. "We'll not eat your food. We have tasted the Bread of Life. Yours would be as gall!" Lisa squeezed her husband's hand in affirmation.

The commander exposed moldy teeth in a grimace. His eyes turned red. He raised his bayonet, preparing to hurl his sword into the brain of this intrepid adversary.

The young soldier stood tall.

The fuming commander thrust forth the gleaming metal, but it instantly plummeted, sideswiped a rock, and clunked uselessly into the muck of the unpaved road. For even as he launched his weapon, upon the youth's head and upon his wife's, there appeared a golden helmet with the word SALVATION.

Recovering his composure, the commander painstakingly led them through the forest into a clearing where a charming log cabin snuggled among shade trees. Nestled against the little cabin, a murmuring, slow-flowing brook teemed with trout, pursuing mouth-watering mayflies and delicious mosquitoes.

Poles and tackle box enticingly lay beside the woven hammock behind the back porch.

The enemy commander bowed low in feigned deference. "It's all yours, ALL yours! Just repose there, luxuriate under the whispering oaks, relish the drifting clouds. Forget your worthless mission."

Husband and wife gazed wistfully into the clearing. It was exactly what they had dreamed of since before their marriage. How had he known?

From an unclouded sky, thunder rumbled its admonition.

The sun's declining afternoon rays hurled a flickering warning, monitory shadows bouncing off white birch and poplar leaves into the shaded yard.

The eagle in the pine stepped unevenly to a lower branch.

David and Lisa looked at each other. They remembered the fabrications offered by this enemy to his commanders, guile designed to entrap and destroy. More subterfuge. Her eyes told him no.

"We don't want your log cabin. We reject it and you. We've a mansion by a river sparkling with eternal life."

As they watched, the beautiful little cottage disintegrated in a burst of blue-hot flames.

With his lips turned up in a sneer of contempt, the commander in black silk snatched a sword from the nearest conscript and hurled it at the young husband's chest. Before it could penetrate flesh, a breastplate materialized upon him and upon his wife. Scribed by divine fire, the word RIGHTEOUSNESS assailed the eyes of the swarthy, raging commander.

Paralyzed with fury, he stood in the mud and twitched nearly out of control. His hawkish eyes rolled and sank, hollow depths of evil.

As the young couple peered into those malevolent orbs, they discerned flames of venom lashing out at the imperious commander's own helpless warriors, who were writhing in irredeemable angst.

The young man saluted the eagle sitting in surveillance. To his wife, he declared, "We will rise up as eagles. We will NOT faint. We will NO LONGER be weary."

David turned to the enemy commander frenzied in his helplessness. "Our weapon is the Word of God, which is sharper than any sword you can brandish against us. Your reign nears its end."

On his hand appeared an open Book with words of truth, powerful and strong, more than sufficient to conquer all the wiles of the dark betrayer.

The eagle, perched on pine branches, stretched its wings as if bestowing an evening benediction, effortlessly ascended, and soared in all its magnificence upward. A soft, affirming light emanated from its majesty.

As lightning crackled across the sky and thunder rocked the earth, the eagle vanished. A new image appeared. Upon a winged stallion sat their Commander, holy, arrayed in resplendent light. With Him a battalion, a cavalry of white-robed followers, sat tall. His eyes beamed unconditional love and unequivocal victory.

The vanquished enemy leader writhed in the mud, babbling incoherently to his men. He possessed no weapons to use against such an offense.

Unafraid and no longer weary, the newly-armed couple turned to leave. They had learned the ways of the enemy, confronted him, and won—in his own territory. Upon their feet, soft sandals etched with the word GOSPEL lifted them victoriously into the presence of their Commander of Love whose name was Omnipotent Eternal God.

A new dawn had come. It was the morning of the seventh day.

Wherefore take unto you the whole armor of God . . .
Stand therefore, having your loins girt about with truth,
and having on the breastplate of righteousness;
and your feet shod with the preparation of the gospel of peace;
above all, taking the shield of faith,
wherewith ye shall be able to quench
all the fiery darts of the wicked.
and take the helmet of salvation, and the sword of the Spirit,
which is the word of God.

Ephesians 6:13-17

Dedicated to Aiden and Peyton—precious PRECIOUS
grandsons.
My greatest desire in this life is that you both will be mighty
warriors for God's Kingdom.

A Tree No Storm Could Conquer

But his delight is in the law of the Lord;
and in his law doth he meditate day and night.
and he shall be like a tree
planted by the rivers of water,
that bringeth forth his fruit in his season;
his leaf also shall not wither;
and whatsoever he doeth shall prosper.

Psalm 1:2, 3

"Choose a spot anywhere on the farm," Dad had offered. "I'll help you plant it."

It was a difficult decision, long considered, for he visualized this little sapling as the most splendid tree in the state, the country, the world! It would be a home for humming birds and robins, a playground for squirrels, perhaps even a place for a great man to seek shelter from life's storms.

"Did yeh give Josh a tree back on his eighth birthday?" Timmy asked his father.

His father nodded and continued to jiggle the carburetor wires on the old John Deere tractor. Timmy understood the silence. It had been in the summer, long ago, about this time of year, that his mother had died. Dad had never been able to talk much about Mom. Timmy tried ever so hard to remember his mother.

He sat on the front porch and patted Chomper, Josh's old mongrel, and pondered.

"Hey, Chomper," he asked. What does a tree need to grow big and strong?"

Chomper responded with a slurpy hand-licking and vigorous tail movement but left Timmy to interpret.

A squadron of black ants marched through the thin-bladed grass at his feet. They seemed to know exactly what they were doing. Timmy thought of Josh, fighting in a war across the ocean. He hoped Josh knew what to do. He missed his older brother.

He thought some more about his tree. Finally, he jumped up and sought his father's hand. Up the hill they trod, up above their small farmhouse. Timmy stopped near the fast-flowing brook at the edge of their property.

"Here, Daddy. It'll get plenty of water and fresh air!"

The wind blew cold and strong as the work-hardened man and the little boy spaded rich, black dirt. With metallic buckets full of stream water they soaked the hole. The child, careful not to injure the roots, inserted the willow seedling and shoveled in the dirt. They packed the soil and stood back to scrutinize its chances.

Mindful to refrain from judging, the man remained impassive, but the child and Chomper raced round and round the prize. Chomper panted hard, his long red tongue bobbing out the side of his mouth.

"See, I'm eight, and the tree and I are just as tall. Which will be bigger next year, Daddy?"

As usual, the child's exuberance made the man chuckle.

In the night a ferocious wind whistled down from the hill above the farmhouse. The little boy snuggled to a shaggy dog never knew that his weary father walked up the hill and sat holding the new growth throughout the storm.

When morning came, Timmy bounded from his bed, dressed, and raced to see if his tree had fared well through the night. All around him fallen branches testified to fury that had whipped the world in anger and died in oblivion. Chomper barked his encouragement all the way.

When Timmy saw his willow droopy, but still upright, drinking in the morning sunlight, he patted the earth and ran to tell his father.

"Daddy, God saved my tree."

His father nodded and smiled. The old tractor putted out to the cornfield.

Later that morning, David came by. "Did ya plant it?" his best friend asked.

"Yep."

"Where?"

"Come on; I'll show you."

They ran in the joy of childhood's strength up the hill.

David scrutinized the withered sapling with a frown. "I'd put it in the valley down yonder," he said as he kicked a pine-cone and catapulted another into the stratosphere. "It'll never live here. Weather's too bad. Too many storms up here."

Timmy didn't agree.

Each morning Timmy raced Chomper to the top of the hill for his daily inspection. Unfailingly, a chipmunk family chattered in outrage. The little tree eased its roots deep into the strength of the earth until it reached the source for the cold stream. There it supped life-giving water. Its dangling branches spread out in rich green, reflecting the bouncing rays of sunlight. Storms no longer threatened the tree.

Timmy sat under his tree and considered his own existence. He thought about his brother.

Distractedly, he watched a tiny ladybug inching toward a drop of water cradled in a web, beauty designed to entrap; once entangled in the invisible threads, the unsuspecting ladybug faced imminent doom. She struggled hopelessly to be free of the terrifying evil approaching her. Only a force supernatural to her world could break those threads that bound her.

Timmy leaned forward. He watched the wicked one advance with eyes focused on its prey, its smile of victory freezing her blood. For the helpless creature, there was no possible escape.

With a broken twig, the young child adeptly snatched the spider and flipped it to the ground, sustaining a painful bite on his heel as he crushed it with his bare foot into the dregs of the earth. The eight-year-old lover of ladybugs released the tiny creature from all her sticky bonds and watched her scurry into freedom.

He thought of Josh, of men hating each other and killing each other. He considered the web. The ladybug needed rescuing from the snare of destruction. So did Josh. So did he.

Stopping only once to rub his sore foot, he ran down the hill with Chomper dancing at his heels.

His father was examining young stalks soon to be heavy with corn. They sat in the sun under floating clouds. With his father's arms on his shoulders, Timmy drank of the rich, cool stream in which flowed the water of eternal life. He experienced the warmth of the Son's love. Like the tree, he would weather the battering of life's storms.

When his ninth birthday arrived, he dashed outdoors ready to measure the willow's growth. He called for Chomper. Timmy called again. Chomper lay by his water dish too weak to rise up. His little black eyes were glazed. His mouth opened to whimper but no sound came out. Timmy screamed for his father.

The vet had been kind. He promised that Chomper wouldn't suffer. It would be over quickly.

On the ride home Dad told Timmy about a man named Job.

Timmy sat under his tree. He'd never known his mother. His big brother was off fighting in the war, and now he'd lost Chomper. He looked up into the tree and saw a mother humming bird, like a tiny helicopter, fluttering above her nest. Clutching his father's worn Bible, he considered Job, the man who'd lost everything he'd treasured and still found breath to praise. Timmy struggled against a blanket of sorrow.

Below him, in a red, woolen workshirt, his father was pounding nails into boards, repairing rotten wood on the tool shed. The hammer strikes echoed upon the hill, like a little dog's coffin pounded shut, like rusty nails pounding and puncturing innocent flesh, pounding into a man spread upon a tree.

Timmy wiped his tears and ran to help. His spiritual roots had begun their growth.

The fever overtook him four weeks before he was ten. In and out of awareness he floated. His father's tired eyes merged in shimmering waves of light and dark. In the distance, Timmy saw Chomper at the base of the hill running up to him but never quite reaching him. In his dream Timmy could not move his legs. He could not descend to Chomper. Then he saw Josh romping with the dog, a halo of light illuminating the darkness of his fever. He sat under his weeping willow, its long green sustaining arms enclosing him. It whispered a gentle song of peace. Timmy slept.

Once he awoke to see David standing in the corner, throwing his old football from hand to hand. Timmy spoke loudly, but his friend didn't seem to hear.

He longed for ice water but was too tired to ask for it. He fell asleep again.

When the fever broke, he rolled over to see his father on his knees beside the bed, head in hands.

"Pop, I'm hungry," Timmy spoke with great effort.

His father looked at him. His face seemed older, haggard. Timmy silently vowed to help more around the farm without being asked.

Tears streamed down his father's face. Timmy wondered why. The room came into focus around him, a room that smelled like the alcohol and peroxide his father had poured on his knee when he was learning to ride a two-wheeler.

"You're in the hospital, Son. It's been a long time."

A young nurse bounced in and put a thermometer in his mouth. She wiped his face with a damp cloth. Another girl in white brought him chicken broth. He wanted a hamburger, French fries, and a Coke. He wondered why he was so weak.

He watched his father's face. A cloud seemed to obliterate the room's sunshine. For some reason he felt a chill of fear.

"Dad, I want to know."

"Tomorrow, Son. You rest now."

The cloud drifted again across his father's eyes.

"Dad ... "

His father hesitated, then pulled up a chair. He struggled for words. He held Timmy's hand.

"I nearly lost you. Now, we're not sure about your legs. You may have trouble walking."

Terror, like a gigantic, cruel whip lashed at his heart, coiled itself around his chest, and squeezed without mercy.

One word explained it all.

"Polio." His father choked as he said the word.

Timmy thought of Chomper collapsing in a heap, his legs weak with disease.

Then he saw the quiet strength and love in his father's eyes. He reflected on the man named Job. He remembered the tree on the hill, where the wind raged, but the tree stood strong with roots probing deep, holding firm in the storms.

His eyes rested on his father's worn Bible. He fell asleep vowing to be strong like the tree. He knew the source of his strength.

Timmy was going home for his birthday. The little nurse who bounced brought him a wheelchair decorated with a big red ribbon and a balloon. He moved into it with difficulty. Therapy had been hard, excessively tiring. "Stretch," they had kindly insisted, again and again and again.

Now he was glad to be going home. David would be there to push him in his wheelchair to the top of the hill. He would find strength to stand, to compare. Which of them had grown more—he or his tree?

Months stretched before him. Each morning he rolled himself to the bottom of the hill within view of his willow. The metal legs of his walker then plopped into the dirt, and he sweated in the morning dew, forcing movement into his legs. He never complained.

On the hill above, the willow wept for him, its hanging branches whispering in the confidence of its strength. "One more step ... Timmy, you can do it ..."

In the field below, his father inspected the bursting kernels of yellow corn and watched, his eyes sad, yet watered with pride.

From the throne, his Heavenly Father sent a cool breeze and watched in love. He saw a boy growing strong against the tempest. He saw a man who would have great influence for Him, a man who would shed tears of joy while casting many crowns at the feet of His Son.

Pain and frustration, overshadowed by a young boy's determined will, step by tiny step, Timmy progressed closer to the tree beckoning him on the hill. The days and months moved slowly.

After the letter came from Josh, Timmy arose even earlier. On the day Josh would be discharged, Timmy would WALK UP THE HILL and they would stand beneath the tree, together refreshed in its shade. Josh would tell him stories about the childhood that he could not remember, about the mother he had barely known. Dad couldn't say the words, but Josh would tell him. Josh would be proud.

Every day Timmy inched his way closer to the tree. He watched robins bearing twigs design a perfect nest, as he daily struggled higher up the hill. He loved the God who taught the robins their craft.

One more day. Josh would be coming home. He stood close enough to touch a lacey branch. Tomorrow, Josh, here beneath this tree, would watch him move away from the legs of metal and lean in his own strength against this trunk.

Timmy slept fitfully. Once in the night he sat bolt upright. An unidentified dread gripped his throat. Uneasiness made him swallow. His mouth was dry.

Morning broke with ominous, dark clouds racing in circles. He'd slept late. No school for him today. Josh was coming home.

He dressed quickly, and balancing on his walker, moved slowly down the hall. The house seemed wrapped in a dismal, bereaved silence.

Timmy entered the living room. A rectangular wooden box draped with an American flag arrested his movement and then his heart. Timmy's breath stopped. His heart fluttered and flipped. He stared, barely comprehending.

His father sat on a chair close to the coffin, staring at an open Bible. Acknowledging Timmy's presence, his father stood, looking at him. Without a word, he prepared the wheel-chair. Timmy understood. This was to be their ceremony, theirs alone. His father pushed him to the bottom of the hill.

With the walker in the dirt, Timmy struggled out of the wheelchair. He looked up at the tree on top of the hill. Its leaves were swirling in the on-coming storm.

Timmy shoved the walker away. He swallowed hard. He moved one leg, then the other. Pain seared his body, as inch by inch, he shuffled up the hill. He didn't feel it. The pain in his heart demanded all of his attention.

He fell. He loved the father who waited quietly and didn't help him get up. He pulled himself to a standing position.

Up they moved. A chipmunk scampered past, scolding them for the intrusion. Timmy watched its agility as it scooted up the trunk of his willow.

The grass parted beneath his dragging, scuffed tennis shoes. The final yard, a little steeper, sapped the last of his energy. Wetness trickled down his cheeks, a bittersweet mixture of sorrow and determined pride.

He was beneath his tree. A few inches more—one more step—his hands moved over the roughness of the willow bark. He leaned against its strength in total exhaustion.

His father stood proud beside him. "It's time I told you about your mother," he said.

The wind roared out of the north. The man and boy stood beneath the weeping willow and stared at the house below. The boy rested against the man and placed his hands also on the worn Bible, into which their spiritual roots had been planted deep and strong. The wind that blew at them without mercy would never be the conqueror.

Therefore whosoever heareth these sayings of mine,
and doeth them,
I will liken him unto a wise man,
which built his house upon a rock:
and the rain descended,
and the floods came, and the winds blew, and it fell not:
for it was founded upon a rock.

Matthew 7:24, 25

Dedicated to Danny—first-born son.
Through every storm of life,
you have emerged stronger as a man of God.
I am unspeakably proud of you.

A Treasure in Her Garden

And let the beauty of the Lord our God be upon us:
and establish thou the work of our hands upon us;
yea, the work of our hands, establish thou it.

Psalm 90:17

G ranny's gift was wrapped in azure-blue polka-dotted paper and tied with a pink-velvet ribbon. Between the dots, pure white lilies smiled out at her. Five packages of seeds, one for each year of her life.

"Small but special, just like you," her grandmother empha-sized. Fresh garden vegetables—multi-colored assorted flowers and to grow on—an odd-shaped bulb, which Granny assured her would burst forth into a wondrous bloom of love, just like the ones on her birthday paper.

Eyes twinkling with amusement, Granny poured the kalei-doscope of shapes into her outstretched chubby palms. "You can never tell what will happen with seeds," Granny twittered. Together they went to till the earth.

Oblivious to the rich, black dirt smudging her cheeks, clinging to her clothes, and creeping under her fingernails, the child knelt, inhaled the fragrance of humus, and deposited the spark of life into uneven little furrows. Here, there, and here again she dropped the seeds while Granny leaned on an old weather-beaten ebony walking stick, and remembering her own first garden, smiled at the euphoria of childhood.

Quickly all the lush, black soil in the tiny garden was planted. She peered up at the wrinkled wisdom beaming down at her and patted her buried treasure just one more time.

Granny paused. "Here, Honey. Here's some soil. Not so good—but dig a hole or two anyway, and there—among the rocks—place a few seeds. Let's see what happens."

Gently the winds blew down the warmth from 93 million miles away and the hurling clouds grew tender as they passed over the child sitting in fertile, black soil, waiting. Softly they bestowed their watery blessing.

"Be patient, Little One. Let God do the work."

Two little eyes squinted up into the sunlight and trusted the wisdom of experience. Still, it wasn't easy to wait.

A millennium passed and another. Tiny white hands grasped the sun-spotted, gnarled, patient ones and tugged. On the well-worn path to the garden, the child wailed, "When, Granny?"

"You can't always see the beginning of a miracle, Child."

It was true. There within the black, naturally-resistant heart of the earth, a tiny structure was germinating—a root, an anchor, a support through which would come the gifts of life. Atop the heart-shaped seed, a little bud, against unbelievably difficult odds had begun its journey to life. UP through the packed earth a sprout was ascending—up to light, up to

God, responding to His call, "Come, come to Me." At His gentle urging, the packed soil fell away, but the triumph would belong to a grandmother and to a small child who would respond to that same lovely urging in her own life.

Her first sprout! How she thrilled over its growth, throughout the day romping over the path to contemplate its progress. Carved blocks of wood once made into castles and hand-sewn, button-eyed dolls lay neglected on the top porch step. The call of life excited her more.

A blossom appeared and a tiny green fruit and finally here and there and over here—in her very own little garden treasures appeared—a carrot patch, some tiny green beans, baby peas, a ripening pink watermelon, a sprinkle of azalea—all joining that beloved first sprout which had turned into the "roundest, orangest, perfectest pumpkin in the whole world" . . . all of them testifying of the One who'd sat upon the horizon and whispered them into being. Granny made sure His part didn't go unappreciated.

In the midst of abundance, Granny's promise of beauty bloomed and captured the heart of a little girl. Up at daylight, the child would perch by the lily and watch it open itself to silently declare its unspeakable blessings.

The child's joy was not without a blot of darkness. The little girl, not having forgotten, often tripped her way to the rocks and to the barren places of less receptive soil. With a tear, she beseeched her grandmother. "Why?"

Granny knew it was a lesson the child must learn. They sat at the window, elbows on white, freshly painted casement and watched. Like a gigantic black shroud, the bug-eyed crow, cackling with victory, descended and gobbled a tiny, helpless seed.

The tenderness of the child was cut through as with a knife and Granny's eyes dimmed with her heartache. The child buried her head in Granny's love. "Some things we can't change, Child. We must plant and leave the rest to God.

The seasons fled by. Yearly, the growing child planted her gardens, while in her own heart the One who gives all life placed the seed of truth in receptive soil. The seed took root and sprouted and the living water descended and the warmth of the Son's love accomplished its work. She knew that gardening would be her lifework.

As the hour came for her departure, she sat the last of many times at a gravestone in a shaft of sparkling sunlight. She placed a radiant, white lily gently on the dark earth. "Lord, tell my grandmother she taught me well. I am ready. I will plant in all kinds of soil, and entrust the harvest to You. And Lord, tell her again, how very much I treasure her." A solitary tear dropped upon the petal's whiteness, clung a moment, descended, and soaked the resting place with love.

Transported to a new land, she prepared to sow seeds. Carefully choosing those appropriate to the soil, she prayed to the Seed-giver.

A young woman bent in grief, bitter with despair over an unfaithful mate, sat in her presence.

"Let this be fertile ground," her heart pleaded. Carefully she opened the Book of Life and told of a Man whose love had ever been constant, a Man who had planted His own body in the earth for three days and then burst forth into a flower so radiant that all might forever inhale his essence and live—and sorrow no more.

Watching the woman's eyes soften and her tears diminish, the young missionary plucked the Lily of the Valley from the Pages of Truth and offered Him.

With her tears, she watered this—her first sprout in this distant land and in the warmth of reflected love, she watched new life begin.

"Seed-giver," sang her heart. "Please tell Grandmother that nothing in this life is better than planting a garden.

*

It wasn't always easy. Her hands grew hard and calloused. Her feet grew thick with miles. Her back bent with the cares of a thousand burdened souls. She knew the Seed she carried was rich beyond all wealth man could imagine. Within it lay the potential for abundant life—and for life-eternal.

Fervently, she climbed the hills and scouted the valleys and planted. Her garden grew beyond her capacity to cultivate. Weeds of discouragement and weariness at times sprang up. She rushed to obliterate the confusion that would strangle new life. Always she watched for the black shroud of the enemy, the ever-hovering crow, his beady eyes ready to detect where he might gobble up her efforts.

She longed for those who might come with strong young hands to pull the weeds and weep with her, giving the Water of Life in this parched land. The harvest cried forth its bounty, grew white with readiness. She had dug the furrows, planted, watered, and weeded. Oh, how she had weeded. Still, some plants withered, for often she worked alone.

Daily, in renewal, she read the Psalm which promised those who "sowed in tears would reap in joy." She firmly believed God had envisioned her, when long ago, He had softly breathed this truth into the soul of His Servant David.

Faithfully she had planted. The wide-eyed orphaned child, asking for Mama. The youthful athlete made paraplegic from a fall—a broken neck. The farmer agonizing over his rice crop flattened by an indiscriminate whirlwind. The rich matron flaunting her jewels by day—groaning of an empty spirit by night.

A thousand lonely souls groveling in the dirt, stirred by the warming call of the Son, filled their empty places with her living Seed. Through the night her tears watered the earthly promise now nearly indiscernible in Grandma's old Bible, ". . . shall doubtless come again rejoicing."

The millenniums of childhood shortened and compressed themselves into moments. She pictured Him more and more clearly. One day, while rejoicing over the harvest of her fields, her vision blurred and grew strangely out of focus. In the midst of the abundance, the Lily which filled her heart metamorphosed before her, and there, surrounding her with His brilliance was the Seed-giver, His eyes melting her soul with eternal promise. She felt an arm around her waist. She didn't have to look to know—it was Granny's.

They that sow in tears shall reap in joy.
He that goeth forth and weepeth,
bearing precious seed,
shall doubtless come again with rejoicing,
bringing his sheaves with him.

Psalm 126:5, 6

Dedicated to Debbie—niece.
I know of no one whose heart has more compassion
for souls than do you.

In the Beginning

When I consider thy heavens,
the work of thy fingers, the moon and the stars,
which thou hast ordained;
what is man that thou art mindful of him?
And the son of man, that thou visitest him?
For thou has made him a little lower than the angels,
and hast crowned him with glory and honor.
Thou madest him to have dominion over the works of thy hands;
thou hast put all things under his feet;
all sheep and oxen, yea, and beasts of the field;
the fowl of the air, and the fish of the sea,
and whatsoever passeth through the paths of the seas.
O Lord, our Lord, how excellent is thy name in all the earth!

Psalm 8:3-9

His mighty hands outstretched, the Great *I Am* stood upon the mountain called Infinity and gazed into its mysterious depths. Only He understood all its secrets. From a distance, adoring winged companions fluttered, watching, breathless with excitement.

Then, so small that only the great and mighty God could see it—upon His upturned hand—there appeared an atomic whirling brain of matter. Again He stretched and reached into nothingness and suddenly around the nucleus flowed miniscule orbiting particles, totally submissive to His command. Thousands and millions of imperceptible revolving galaxies gathered upon His palm. The dust of the Earth had begun to exist.

As He raised His hand with a flinging movement, a thousand-million granules scrambled through space, chaotically seeking one another, until the voice of His will ended their confusion and they formed a planet called Earth, where one day He would walk in obscurity; He would walk and love and die and rise again—and return in victory.

In response to his voice, a tiny spark of light began to glow until, upon the lazily spinning planet below, there came a division of light and dark. The primal earth rolled obediently in its appointed course. As the new planet neared the end of its first momentous journey, the King of Glory sat in the midst of praise, enveloping each beloved worshiper with agape love.

On the second day there would be separation of waters—there would be sea and there would be mists in the heavens. The beloved host waited; with eager devotion they waited. Again transported through space by love, the excited spectators fluttered and whirled, waited and watched.

On the mountain called Infinity, He stood again, in silence, hearing the clank of chains that would for a time enslave men's hearts. A mighty tear dropped upon the gathering dust. It enclosed the pristine land in sizzling mists, shrouded it in darkness. Then across the eons of time, as He listened, there echoed the piercing blows of a merciless hammer striking rusty nails. He considered fragile souls. He would not make men puppets, but would draw them with His life-changing love. With tenderness, He watched the sphere tumbling in its appointed orbit below.

The Spirit hovered, brooding, encircling, approving.

The Father on the throne lowered His head. In that moment He visualized the thorns and spikes upon the roses, the mangled bodies of innocent lambs, a garbage dump outside the Holy City from whence one day He would turn His face— that He might not see the refuse of the world's wickedness piled recklessly upon the purity of His Son. At the same time, He remembered the future celebration, when the multitudes who had bathed in eternal joy, would stand unblemished in His presence. They would sing of amazing grace.

Father, Son, and Holy Spirit focused their gaze upon sacrificial, holy hands, trembling, mangled, spread wide upon a splintered tree. Alpha and Omega knew the beginning and the end, eternity past and future. Somewhere in the midst of created time, between the eternal before and the eternal thereafter, the ticking of Earth's clock toward Calvary had begun.

The water of his mighty tear covered the Earth. Great fogs and mists restlessly roamed, blocking out light. The angels, remembering the pure river flowing from the throne, realized that water meant life, for they had heard the Son when He declared: "Whosoever drinketh of the water that I shall give him shall never thirst."

The Giver of Life approached the teeming particles of dust and with a prodigious breath whispered life-sustaining atmosphere into space, caught it, shaped it, and patted it gently around the planet, a transparent atmosphere, that men might peer through it into infinite space with telescopes and marvel. He scooped up sparkling droplets of water and finger-painted them into a great cloud canopy. He smiled at the adoring host and beckoned them.

Hilarity shattered the blueness as ten thousand times ten thousand joyous, frolicking servants jumped and bobbed in the fluffy ocean of cloud. The Creator of All Things laughed, leaned His elbow upon the canopy of air and waited, that it might accurately be written, "And the evening and the morning were the second day."

As the third orbit began, the Creator arose and approached his day's work radiant with expectancy. Today there would be new life. The playful seraphim quieted and assumed resting positions upon the clouds: some were sitting; some were reposing face down—their extremities designing snow angels in the billows; others reclined on their sides; but all were intent; all were electric with excitement.

The Great One stood upon the waters and breathed cool-ness into the Earth's thin silicate crust. With His fingers He traced a massive ocean and stirred its currents into motion. Gently probing under the crust, He nudged out volcanic islands. Again reaching below the crust into Earth's mantle, He buckled the land, fashioning continents, adorning them with imposing mountain peaks and rippling valleys.

Then upon the barrenness, He stirred black soil. From his lips emerged a tiny seed, and another, and another, each infused with the gift of reproducing life. Into a shallow furrow He placed a germinating bud. He called the wind and it gently blew. He summoned the heat and it warmed the seed. At his bidding, the mist soaked its encouragement. In just a whisper of time, as the Designer beckoned them, millions of sprouts burst forth, up into the light, to proclaim themselves wondrous miracles of His creativity.

Single-celled diatoms (500 in a drop of water), giant sequoias, kelp lounging sleepily in the sea, bearded mosses, shy mountain violets, cone-bearing junipers, wild mustard bushes, the olive, the papyrus, the shrub bearing the gift of frankincense, the medicinal myrrh tree, the symbolically-adoring palm with its waving branches and leaves, the blue herb called hyssop—that day they would be joined by thousands of their kind—designed to reach up to light, up to Him, for as long as man would inhabit the Earth.

At his call, the angels, like a huge company of paratroopers, floated to the land. Each given a handful of seeds, a day's supply, they tripped and skipped all over the Earth. One by one they deposited seeds. They lingered for the nurturing. For the Lord God knew that each new life would always need attending.

As each tiny seed struggled in its journey through the impenetrable darkness, the angel waited; and then as emerald velvet burst through the dew-softened soil, attesting again to his glory, the angel proclaimed in sweet song, "Alleluia to our King." Before long, the whole Earth was trembling with the vibrations of angelic rejoicing. Verdant life appeared everywhere as his glorified servants planted, waited, rejoiced. Finally the last seed was planted; the last green sprout appeared.

With an all-embracing voice, the Great Creator issued the command, "Reproduce with seeds, after your own kind." In his mind He saw twelve chosen seeds—chosen not because they were rich or physically attractive, or particularly good, or humanly significant—but chosen simply because He loved them. He saw those human seeds reproducing and nurturing a rock-strewn barren land of souls so that every tongue and nation could one day be offered Truth. His heart overflowed with love.

The song softened. His winged planters, resting on green carpet, inhaled the sweet fragrance of apple blossoms from a central garden He named Eden.

Soon it was the morning of the fourth day. From their places upon the solidness of the Earth's crust, the angels gazed through the great encircling cloud and waited.

His gentle eyes beamed a command. At first upon his hand there appeared a muted glow, which magnified and sparkled and bounced and obediently rolled itself into a mighty ball of gas and splashing flame, powerfully hurling forth a spray of heat and light in every direction.

Reaching beyond space with his other hand, He plucked a tiny bit of nothingness and rolled it lovingly, deliberately between his fingers. One by one, giant particles exploded into existence. With his fingers He carefully adjusted their distance from the great convulsive, burning energy. Gently He tapped them, as might a child in game of marbles. And so into their destined orbits these regal particles nestled, ready to twinkle forth his excellence, quite willing to declare the glories of God.

The celestial chorus, thrilled with the spectacle, resounded its adulation into the farthest corners of the universe, a melodious incense inhaled by the swirling Spirit of God.

Upon the throne the Father smiled and proclaimed that it was good.

The Son beamed the light of love into every angelic heart.

To some of the newly formed planets, the Creator affectionately presented tiny, spinning companions—to the Earth He gave but one. To some He gave magnificent crowns of multicolored rings. The Son knew that one day men with limited vision would peer through gigantic telescopes and ponder the beginning of such things. Some of them would neither comprehend nor admit that crowns far more magnificent than any seen in the earthly sky were available for the claiming, crowns indestructible, incorruptible.

As darkness walked around the Earth, the King of All Things flung twinkling lights into the sky, first a fixed Northern light to guide man's explorations, then a tiny dipper, and a larger one. The angels remembered dipping freely into the river of life and enjoying its abundance.

Then laughing with resplendent delight, the Lord God appeared in the midst of his adoring angelic companions, his arms filled with dazzling brilliance. In one mighty movement He tossed it up and out and a billion tiny lights in a billion galaxies laughed back until even the dignified archangel Michael rolled over on his back and chuckled.

The King of Laughter stood upon the Earth. He picked up a handful of sand and watched the granules slip through His fingers. In a thundering voice He announced, "It shall be written that the stars number as the sand of the sea." All around Him, his servants marveled and adored. They listened to the melodies of the stars. The Creator thought of a man named Job, his servant, who would proclaim 4000 years before man's science even considered it, "The morning stars sang together."

The Lord transformed the star beams into a giant harp and softly stroked the strings of light. The angels sang, mingling their voices with the music from the seven corners of space, exalting Him. The Creator gazed with love upon his devoted servants as they sang in sublime euphony. The Earth, meanwhile, rolled around, completing its fourth orbit.

The sun whirled its rays 93 million miles into the fifth day. The angels scrambled for their designated positions. He stood upon the water and knew that one day in his humility He would walk upon these waves and a man named Peter would grow in faith. He reached down into the water, which was to be called the Sea of Galilee. As He pulled away his hand, a thousand tiny fins gulped their first taste of life. Color, movement, excitement filled the seas everywhere, multitudes of shapes and hues, all exalting his majesty—a different fish dedicated to each angelic being.

Absorbed in the wriggling rainbows in the water, his eager servants nearly missed the next explosion of color and song. In the sky over all the Earth, the twitters and peeps and cuckoos announced the arrival of new grandeur.

The triune God watched and laughed as winged servants splashed in the waters—riding the giggling porpoises, tickling the yet-gentle sharks—others soared in the playful wind—

swooping with the eagles, gliding with the hawks, fluttering with the tiny humming birds.

In frolicsome mimicry, a rosy-cheeked cherub shuffled with a pair of tuxedoed king penguins. The Lord God knew that men, likewise, would find infinite pleasure in the companionship of his creatures.

As the fifth day neared its end, all of creation sensed something even more remarkable was to occur. Soon it would be the sixth day.

In great families He made them. Cats of every size and description strolled and stretched sleepily, yawing in the sun. Dogs, hyenas, wolves, yipping and woofing, wagged their tails, eagerly seeking to spread affection. Big blacks and tiny koala bears rumbled and grinned their way into every awestruck angelic heart. Lizards, dinosaurs, and big-mouthed crocs assigned to aerate the soil brought laughter as they yawned and squiggled in luscious mud. When an eccentric duck-billed, fur-covered platypus waddled into a river on his little knuckles, and with his droll beaver tail, splashed a swarthy toad napping on a lily pad, hilarity erupted.

The angels delighted in each new creature until the earth was filled with life—in the sea, in the air, and now on the land. The seraphs could only marvel at His infinite creativity.

They focused their eyes and detected multitudes of mini-creatures even in one drop of water. It seemed that the Great Creator would never stop. Each new life savoring its debut in the unblemished freshness of the sixth day brought murmurs of amazement and pleasure to the onlookers. Male and female—two of each—commanded to multiply and fill the earth, nuzzling each other, wobbled or waddled or hopped or bounded away.

The Spirit whirled again, surrounding the Earth with his loving approval.

Then from the throne, the majestic Father stood, even as He would one day stand to welcome home his martyred friend Stephen. The sovereign Father stood, anticipating the paramount achievement of this—the sixth day.

By silent command, all of creation hushed. The gentle wind obediently tucked itself into billowy clouds. The fish snuggled into quiet waters, listening, watching the reflection in the mirror of sky. Soaring birds found convenient branches and nestled close. The curious land animals instinctively formed a gigantic circle.

The Great Lord of the Universe looked around exultantly at all He had made. For a moment He concentrated in perfect communication with the hovering Spirit and with the Father. Together the Trinity declared approval. It was good, indeed!

A white tiger rolled over in the heat. The Lord of All smiled, walked over and scratched his tummy. The fat, gray toad, now bathing her warts in a warm puddle, rolled her bug eyes at her mate and burped happily. A male peacock strutted, his rainbow tail shivering in the eyes of his appreciative wife.

The entire universe watched and waited.

Noticed only by the Lord, a serpent of unspecified origin flicked its forked tongue in the direction of the King of Love and slithered surreptitiously across an open place and out of sight.

Time and eternity paused.

Then the omnipotent God positioned Himself upon the dust and raised his hands; every living thing watched and waited in deferential silence. The crowning glory of all creation was about to appear.

Down He reached and scooped up a ball of mud. Gently He molded and caressed the clay. His eyes tender with emotion, the Lord of the Universe opened his hands and placed Adam blinking upon the dewy greenness.

"It's not all that great," thought the mammoth elephant. I'm far stronger."

"Look at its puny legs," pondered the cheetah. "I can run much faster." He stretched himself confidently in the sun.

"I'm far more beautiful. Why does He seem to cherish it so?" wondered the Hyacinth macaw. He fluttered his brilliant blue wings hoping to draw a few admiring glances.

To every life drawn into this moment by the Lord of the Universe, it was obvious that this new creation, called man, was uniquely precious. The angels, long the objects of His eternal affection, understood unconditional love. Because He loved this new creation so much—though they were not certain why—they loved him also.

Then the Lord God spoke. "Let us make man in our image." Father, Son, and Holy Spirit—the Triune God—stooped to breathe his essence into Adam. Intellect, will, emotion. He gave Adam spirit that he, he and his descendants only, could communicate in reciprocal love—that redeemed man could worship God in a way incomprehensible even to the angels.

As the Eternal Word, gazing upon this precious creature, prepared to present him with a wife, only He was cognizant of just how precious man was and the price to be paid for his eternal freedom.

The hissing serpent of undesignated origin slithered again through the open space under the Banyon tree.

The Lord God of Creation gazed upon the tree which harbored the knowledge of good and evil. He saw, instead, a tree upon a distant hill called Calvary. Turning His focus upon Adam, God began to speak.

It would be written that the morning and the evening were the sixth day.

For by him were all things created,
that are in heaven,
and that are in the earth.

Colossians 1:16

Dedicated to Joan—daughter-in-law.
You absolutely love life and beauty and creativity.
I can picture you laughing with the angels,
but . . . hushing as your King raises His hand for the
next miracle.
Then, as always, I can hear the praise from your lips.

... and in loving memory of your precious mom ...
now laughing with the angels.

Audrey Snyder

When the Time Was Right

Bless the Lord, O my soul,
O Lord my God, thou art very great;
thou art clothed with honor and majesty.

Psalm 104:1

O nce there was a mighty king who lived in a distant galaxy in a kingdom so beautiful, that if a traveler by chance could have entered in, he would have paused in awe and gasped in wonder.

This king was known far and wide and everywhere, for his love and justice could not be matched. The king's heart was filled with joy as he loved and talked and walked through the lovely land. Pure transparent gold reflected his beauty and rays of rainbow-colored lights accompanied him. As he traversed his kingdom, softly-swaying palm branches eagerly whispered "Hosanna." Celestial music like millions of perfectly tuned instruments from every part of the universe announced his coming and the creatures of his domain fell prone before him—adoring.

While the king's eyes radiated love, an observant onlooker could detect that not ALL was well in the king's heart. Though his kingdom was perfect and love reigned, from somewhere in another galaxy, the king heard a sighing. "*El Shaddai . . .*"

And he knew that he was needed. But the time was not yet.

From nothingness the king had plucked every color of precious, transparent jewel that he might design the foundations of his city—the diamond called jasper, the blues of sapphire and chalcedony, the green of the emerald, red and white of sardonyx and sardius, the gold of crysolyte, the sea-green of beryl, the golden-yellow of imperial topaz, the violets and rich purples of jacinth and amethyst. His decorations were breathtaking.

Inspecting the jasper walls of his golden domain, the king noted with satisfaction the twelve jeweled foundations upon which he had inscribed twelve names: Simon who is called Peter; Andrew his brother; James the son of Zebedee; John his brother; Philip; Bartholomew; Thomas; Matthew the Publican; James the son of Alphaeus; Thaddeus; Simon the Zealot; and Matthias—for he had already chosen them.

So it was that he surveyed and governed his kingdom. His presence lighted and adorned his capital city. About the size of the moon it was, a perfect square. Its denizens lived not upon this cube, as we live upon the Earth, but on levels and levels of beautiful, transparent streets in mansions of clear gold. There the inhabitants never wept, never argued, never gossiped behind closed doors, never inflicted harm. More than two million square miles of space—room for thirty times as many people as now live on our globe.

The king knew that his joyful realm was good. The Tree of Life, transplanted from a distant garden called Eden, produced abundant fruit. The river of sparkling clear water flowed from beneath his throne unthreatened by pollutants. The roses never withered. The patriarchs never grew older. The lambs bounded over the landscapes free from fear. The lion and the lamb rollicked in fragrant meadows while the king watched and laughed. But in his laughter there was not only joy. For afar in another galaxy, the king still heard the sighing. "*El Elyonna Adoni...*"

He knew that he was needed, but the time was not yet.

The slightest movement—and the walls glittered and flashed with majestic beauty. All celestial activity paused. A hush—for all were choked with inexpressible emotion. Somewhere a whisper, then a murmur... "Worthy, W O R T H Y ..." The song magnified and the crescendo surged, shaking the very walls of the kingdom as the multitudes celebrated TRUTH. The Author of Truth was listening and loving, yet, still, he heard a sighing from afar. "*Yahweh...*"

But the time was not yet.

Then one day the king fashioned a gate of transparent pearl into the sparkling wall. He labored alone, though he could have commissioned 10,000 eager assistants, with but a whisper. The angelic host watched as the king travailed. Great drops of sweat rolled down his cheeks. He paused and said to his beloved, "This is my burden only, for this gate of pearl is forged at great price."

To the onlookers it appeared that the king's own perfect purity emerged, as if his very own essence had issued forth, coating a particle of something very dark and unpleasant from an unknown distant place, layer upon layer, until the elegance of that magnificent pearl radiated the king's glory, sculptured into a gate that would never be closed.

The king appeared to be thinking of something momentous. His heart seemed far away from the loveliness of this kingdom. For, only he could hear the far-off sighing. *"Jehovah . . ."*

The time was soon. But it was not yet. Time for him to build eleven more gates of pearl and upon the twelve gates, he inscribed names: Benjamin, Ephraim, Manasseh, Naptali, Dan, Asher, Issachar, Judah, Zebulon, Simeon, Reuben, and Gad.

"JEHOVAH . . ."

The Omniscient One could perceive it all—past, present, and future. He grieved, with transcendent love, for those who sighed . . . but the time was not yet.

The good and mighty king continued his reign. The sweet fragrance of jasmine and sweeter still the incense of prayer surrounded his steps. The TRUTH of his Word anointed every living entity, while his subjects marveled at omniscience. The caressing, compelling light called LOVE gently filled every corner of his city and infinitely beyond into far-flung space, as from his heart unconditional love radiated.

But the king's preoccupation was becoming infectious. Something was soon to happen. The king, still listening to the sound of sighing, finally allowed the residents of the city also to hear. Among the sighs, they heard "*Messiah . . . M e SIGH a h.*"

The king walked to the gate of pearl. Father, Son, and Spirit—mysterious, indescribable, unfathomable Trinity—communed in perfect love.

And then he knew it was time.

Michael appeared at his bidding. One by the one, the king removed the robes of kingship. He laid them on Michael's outstretched arms. He removed his golden crown. He stood before all in his humility. Yet they fell prone in worship, for not one in this place doubted for a moment his eternal worthiness. "It is time to finish this gate," was all he said.

Off into space he stepped.

When consciousness returned, the great king had "made of himself no reputation and had taken upon himself the form of a servant and was thus made into the likeness of men."

He rested briefly in the arms of an obscure virgin maiden; beside her knelt a devoted young Jewish carpenter. It was no accident that the One who had constructed a perfect city, twelve gates of pearl, and an entire universe apprenticed himself to this young carpenter. Even before the king had visualized the jeweled foundations of his kingdom, he had chosen these two, whose hearts receptive to eternal Truth, would also gladly nurture Agape Love.

He walked among men, but they would not bow, for their noses were sniffing for material things and did not catch the sweet aroma of the king. Their eyes were seeking after the lusts of the flesh and would not see his light. Their ears were listening for gossip and steps to power over other men; they did not hear the celestial orchestra that still played.

It was often said of the king that he wept.

As he walked among men, he saw their pain, saw them curse the way, the truth, the life, the light, the crystal-clear water from the throne, the lion that playfully romped with the lamb. As they struggled for elusive power lasting but a moment, he saw them inflict pain, saw them die. He touched them with his hands, his words—with life, with power. Still they would not open their eyes, their ears, nor their hearts.

He walked among the sighing men.

"And being found in fashion as man, he humbled himself and became obedient unto death, even the death of the cross."

*

Two millenniums later men still sigh. There are those who recognize the resurrected, restored King. They call him Jesus. He calls them His bride. While they wait patiently to behold their King face to face, they dream of the gate of pearl, of entering His city, of glorifying, adoring, and enjoying the King forever. They wait for Him to say, "The time is now." And they remember the price He paid.

Who being in the form of God,
thought it not robbery to be equal with God:
but made himself of no reputation,
and took upon him the form of a servant,
and being found in fashion as a man,
He humbled himself,
and became obedient unto death,
even the death of the cross.
Wherefore God also hath highly exalted him

and given him a name which is above every name:
that at the name of Jesus every knee should bow . . .

Philippians 2:5-10

Dedicated to Pastor David Uth, First Baptist
Church of Orlando.
Every Sunday morning you unveil another
glimpse of King Jesus.
Thank you for your faithfulness.

. . . And Then, Through the Gate

Let us be glad and rejoice, and give honour to him:
for the marriage of the Lamb is come, and his wife hath
made herself ready.
And to her was granted that she should be arrayed in
fine linen, clean and white:
for the fine linen is the righteousness of the saints.
And he saith unto me, Write,
Blessed are they which are called unto the marriage
supper of the Lamb.

Revelation 19:7-9

S he hadn't believed in love at first sight until she saw him, perched there on his decrepit wooden throne. The glowing afternoon sun reflected in his wavy, platinum hair and appropriately crowned him with all of its glory.

His alert lifeguard eyes surveyed the people polka-dotting the shoreline. She reflected upon a regal father lion, king of his domain, stretching under the sun, flexing his powerful legs, ever watchful of his cubs tumbling near the waterhole. From a book she'd loved reading as a child, she called to mind a magnificent lion named Aslan of Narnia.

Was it destiny that drew her to this moment? To him? Or was it something even greater than destiny? From her place on the hot sand below his lifeguard station, she looked up and saw a unique tenderness in his eyes and heard an unmatched compassion in his words as he cautioned the children into safety.

She felt compelled to move to him, as if all of eternity past and present had prepared her for this encounter. She adjusted her new suit—for her, a bit flamboyant in shocking pink and purple swirls—but selected specifically for such a moment as this. Would he notice her? Would he also be drawn into the destiny of this moment?

She fluffed her hair and moved purposefully into his line of vision. But before she could utter a word, she heard a cry of alarm from the curling breakers. Sand whipped across her legs, stinging, causing her to lurch awkwardly, as her yet unnamed beloved brushed past her sprinting toward the surging, foaming swells.

In the water a small boy and his sister, snatched by an unheralded undertow, were being swallowed up within tongues of liquid death. Two little heads bobbed; arms flailed; mortal terror reigned.

Into the blue-green depths he plunged, his powerful arms stretching his humanness toward unpredictable treachery.

In horror she bolted, tripping through the sand, to the water's edge.

Through the ghostly grayness he moved, her golden lion king powerful in his youth, confident, purposeful. A few skilled strokes brought him quickly into the current of death. He was there with the tiny victims, holding them, knowing their weakness, sharing their fate. He was talking to them. Their panic obviously subsided, for the wild thrashing ceased.

From the shore, she could detect no fright in him. He appeared not to struggle against the insistent pressure clutching his legs. With his infinite wisdom and compassion, he had calmed the terror; he had merely hitchhiked a ride upon the current, floating L-shaped toward the shore a half mile away. The muted crowd began to babble as they dashed excitedly toward the place of rescue. A siren wailed ever closer, undulating a sympathetic howl.

The spectators applauded his act of heroism; then dispersed, grateful for fresh dinner conversation. The young mother cuddling her restored treasures, pronounced her benediction, and then the ambulance whisked her away into grateful memory.

Only she was left.

Still dripping, he stood looking at her, contemplating her seriousness. Suddenly he broke into a hearty laugh. She tingled in the sweet aroma of the sound.

Then he spoke, "Come. Walk a bit and talk with me."

His gentleness fell upon her. His smile wrapped itself around her shoulders and propelled her. They sat in the sand. His words, unlike any she'd ever heard spoken by man, wisdom beyond earthly grasp, drew her mind and then her heart. For some reason she felt that he had always loved her.

Above them, a mighty Artist dipped his paintbrush into magenta and blushing pink. They watched as He stroked brilliance across the earth's blue vault. Into the darkening horizon the evening star sneaked, unnoticed, a benevolent chaperone, twinkling down its approval. The young lovers shared their souls. The big dipper puffed heart-shaped clouds, like a small child gaily blowing bubbles. But the young hero and the girl sitting on the beach barely noticed.

Each day when the factory whistles tooted their afternoon release, she covered her shiny new electronic typewriter and tidied up her desk. She headed for the emerald sea roaring its unpredictability and the sleek youth who had conquered it and her. Summer days stretched lazily ahead of them.

He lay with chin resting upon cupped hands and teased a sand crab idiotically fleeting its shadow. "Here, little fellow, go that way," he gently admonished and turned to gaze at her.

She hesitated. Fearful of his answer, her heart quickened and even fluttered a little as she inquired, "What will you do when summer is over and the whirling leaves tempt the children from the beach and the skies fill with wintry bluster?" She had finally asked.

He rolled over on his back to read the message in the clouds. He reached out and touched her trembling fingers. He seemed to know, that hearing his answer, she would need more than words.

"I must go away."

Sorrow convulsed from deep within her and forced itself out and down her cheek. He wiped it away. The back of his tawny hand lingered softly upon her tears. She gasped with the powerful gentleness of his touch. She closed her eyes to inhale the memory.

Nearby gulls squawked in dispute over a piece of dry bread. The real world hadn't gone away. In the distance a sorrowful siren reminded her again of life's frailty, of joy's shortness.

Then he spoke again. "I must save the world." His boyish sparkle, his captivating impishness still peeked through the seriousness in his eyes.

She spoke. "But here, you have rescued two."

"It is not enough."

A chilling wind puffed across the beach. The days were growing shorter. The children turned their eyes toward the many beckoning hues of autumn leaves piled just high enough for jumping.

Finally he said, "I will see you tomorrow at daybreak."

As the morning star floated through the brightening sky, he arrived. "Come, let me show you my garden. Let me show you what I have created." He laughed happily. "I think you'll agree it's very good."

There it was. The rose. They lingered to admire the mossy redness of the dew-soaked bloom. She inhaled crimson fragrance. Her heart clung to the love she saw in his eyes.

Again she whiffed the fragrance of the rose for a glorious moment. She thought of the multitudes that had never held a rose. She considered herself most fortunate.

Next to the rosebush he stood with her. A daddy-long-legs had strung his invisible threads, all through the night weaving an intricate pattern, for the millionth time testifying to the existence of a Great Designer. "Look," he said, fully enjoying her appreciation.

Tiny droplets glistened and clung, awaiting the morning heat. Through the prism a rainbow formed, a promise in miniature. She laughed again and supped the nectar of his presence.

They drove to the mountain that reigned over the kaleido-scope of autumn, daily challenging the colors of the sunset in friendly competition. They stood upon the summit. A blushing white-tailed deer peeked around a myrtle bush, eavesdropped for a moment, and then bounded demurely over a fallen maple. She admired the effortless beauty of his leap. She remembered the rose and the sparkle in the web. "Your garden is glorious."

"I love it also. But to me you are more beautiful. I love you far more."

She knew that today he would leave.

They stood at the top of the mountain and watched the frisky wind scoop a pile of red and orange leaves and flip them carelessly into a motley carpet.

His arms encircled her waist. He held her close and kissed her tears, his own mingling with hers. He reached into his pocket and pulled out a velvety purple box and opened it. A magnificent pearl ring glimmered in the sunlight.

"Wear this until I come for you," he pleaded. "I promise I will come for you. Will you dress in white and wear my pearl and wait for me?"

He had guarded the beaches. Now he would guard the skies. He would soar through the vaulted blueness and chase the enemy. The children could play freely in the waves, in the swirling leaves, in the billowing white bluster of winter. Her pilot, roaring like a lion in the sky, would be the best. He would be their savior. Her eyes clung to him.

"I will wait for you," she promised.

Then he was gone.

*

Each morning she awoke with the star that had blessed them. She paused to admire the rose and the dew-sprinkled web. She closed her eyes and inhaled the memory of love. Then the factory whistles tooted their demands. The real world would not be ignored.

She walked in the world, yet no longer seemed a part of it. For upon her finger the opalescent pearl rested, her ever-present reminder that He would keep His promise. She found herself dressed in white, prepared always. Perhaps this day He would come.

In the distance, rumors of wars rumbled. She looked to the sky. Would He come today?

A needy child cried in the street without direction. She was there. To her bosom she grasped the abandoned, the discouraged, the bereaved. Wherever sorrow randomly intruded to torment helpless victims, she was there. "If you look in the right place, you will find Love," she promised.

She showed them the rose. "The thorn is sharp, but the beauty is stronger."

She showed them the sparkling, dewy webs. "The prism reflects every color of love. Look for the promise within the prism," she pleaded.

In the distance, wars like ugly volcanoes of fire suffocated and destroyed.

"Forget the pearl ring," taunted the crowd.

"He's dead," shouted one.

"He's forgotten you," exclaimed another.

She clung to the ring and watched the heavens.

An orphaned child clung to her fingers. They stooped to pet two tawny kittens, little lions content in the heat. They had stretched themselves over a warm, smooth log and fallen asleep, oblivious to perilous times.

As the child stroked the softness of their innocence, she noticed the pearl ring.

"It's a promise that He will come again," she explained. Then she told about a love so perfect and pure that the child easily understood and announced, "I want that kind of love in my life also."

How long had it been since she had touched His hands, heard the melody of His words? The world had known earthquakes, the terror of a reactor-meltdown, pestilences in the blood, serial killers, uprisings, bloody confrontations between brothers. Dirges clamored for attention. Through the grief she walked, clutching the children to her side, comforting the sob-wrenched widow, reminding all that Love was stronger than the funeral song. The pearl glistened on her hand.

Early one morning, seeking refreshment, she retreated to the mountain summit. She rested near a blood-red rose-bush, which was laced with intricate rainbow webs. From her pocket she pulled a well-worn letter, of love and promise. She'd memorized every line, but seeing the words always brought Him closer.

"In a twinkling... when you don't expect me... I will come again... that where I am there you may be also."

In the distance she heard music, a song so lovely that she began to tremble, wondering if it could be He. She stood to hear more clearly. Suddenly she realized it was indeed the voice of her Beloved singing a song of love so magnificent that no human heart could have imagined it. She wondered if it was his friend Michael, or perhaps Gabriel, who was playing the trumpet as He sang.

She ran in the direction of the vibrations that surrounded the mountain. Though she was running, the movement seemed effortless; her feet glided above the earth. Then she heard Him laugh. Faster she moved until all the marvelous beauties of earth—that kaleidoscope of color and sound that she loved—mingled, thrilling her senses.

And then–there He was! His arms were about her and their laughter echoed into infinite space. He handed her a rose, scarlet, like blood.

"I've come just as I promised."

She experienced a rapture never before known by human heart.

Color surrounded their joy—the rose, autumn flipping and flashing its splotches on the excited wind, the brushstrokes of the morning sun suffusing glory upon the eastern sky, and the bouncing reflection of a rainbow exuding its promise as it peeked from little prisms in the gossamer web. But the greatest beauty came from the color of their love.

Her tears flowed. "You've been wounded," she cried.

His hands, His head, His side, though healed, bore the marks of grievous suffering.

He grasped her hands with joy. "It's over. Today is your wedding day. Come away with me."

He transported her to the home He'd prepared. As they stood before the entrance, she looked first upon the gate and then upon her hand. Her pearl ring sparkled. Somehow it had become the gate—adorned now for her, as for the most treasured of brides.

Her Beloved stood in the opening and beckoned her. "Come. In the secret places of the stars will I see your face."

She stepped through the gate of pearl into Eternal Love.

My voice shalt thou hear in the morning, O Lord;
in the morning will I direct my prayer unto thee, and
will look up.
Psalm 5:3

Dedicated to Sue, Terry, Noell, Laurie, Lisa,
and Marilyn—my friends.
You consistently live the faithful life and
watch always for the King.

and

To Lissie—niece.
Have we ever had a conversation not sprinkled liber-
ally with the awe of who He is?
With you – daily I worship!
There is no greater gift a human can give to me.

Acknowledgement of God's inexpressible blessings!

God blesses us through the gift of family and friends
and His faithful servants who present Truth.
For you, oh how I give thanks!

I thank God for a lifetime of incredible gifts—my
extended family.

Myrtle and Ted.
Denise and Eldon.
Michele and Bob—Terri—Chris, Jeremy, Joshua; Sandy and
Bobby; Don; Bobby and Ruth—Lacey, Michaela, Stephanie,
and Brent.
Nicole and Dave—Amelia.
Elise and Joe—Joseph and Jonathan.
Greg and Suzanne—Josh and Sharon, Cody, Corrie, and Caleb;
Jenny; Zachary.
Bob and Sabre.
Bill and Jackie.

Glenn and Dorthy.
Dortha.
Ruth.
Bob—Bobby, Jimmy, and Paul.

Arnold and Jean—Debbie; Dan and Carol—Glenn and Julie—
Eisen, Landon, Charis; Jenny and Alan—John Daniel; Kim
and Stephen—Elijah, Layla; Steve and Nettie—Jessica, Curtis,
Justin; Dortha and Mark—David and Rachel.

*

God gave each of you to me as a gift of friendship
wrapped in His love.

Kaye, Eunice, Judy, Doris, Nancy, Carol.
Manoogian, Crump, John, Francie, Sue and Bill.
Sandy and Bob.
John K., Whitney, Pindar, Taylor, Gayarre, Gowdie, Medina, Lee,
Okie.
Sherry, Mark, Donna, Dave B., Alice, Kari, Chuck, AJ., Gary, Janet,
Noell, Robert, Ken and Nancy, Jackie and Paul, Jeff and Heather,
Ludwig, Hofman, Mulder, Patino, Dann, Pappas, Maffet,
Dieleman, Jezequell, Scott, Nolander, Stones, Levi, Hathaway,
Mayfield, Ritsema, VanderWoude, Medder, Wooten, Wyss,
Doc, Joel, Diane, Janet, Karen, Donna, Lynell, Jen, Jane, Beth,
Cheryl, Bianca, Patti, Claudia, Laura, Kristen, Bev, Marilyn, Rob,
Shannon, Marjorie, Lee, Yeni. Robert, Arlene, Emil, Chris V.
Terry and Charles.
Laurie, Kammi, Lisa, Michael, Jim, Patti, Richard, Doug, Anthony,
Dolly, Jessica, Jan, Pete, Molly, Darren, Jennifer, Kathryn, Vicky,
Debbie, Cindy, Ulysses, Trish, Alan, Caroline, Julie, Jeff, Samuel,
Elizabeth, Jan, Brian, Reinhold.
Pete and Helena, Patricia and Hendrick .
Steve Lash-Blue Book Cars.
John Ripley-Fellowship Financial.

The WCS class of 2002, for your special gift to me.

The OCS class of 2011, for your laudable attitude and effort.

Hundreds of precious students through the decades.

—I could not, on my own, find more precious friends.

For His servants, whose words and actions have profoundly impacted my life, I thank God.

I especially appreciate the following:

Lyle Green and Ann, Bob King and Marilyn, Rod Evans and Pat, David Hughes and Lisa, Brad Stephenson, Jim Bruton and Oleta, Jimmy Knott, David Uth, Dr. Dan Yachter—as you heal our bodies, you reveal His love and power, and my new friend Ramona.

*

Through the airwaves and in the written word, God has gifted us with the opportunity to sit at his feet.

I especially appreciate the following:

WTLN 950 AM Orlando Florida

Ravi Zacharias, David Jeremiah, Charles and Andy Stanley, Chuck Swindoll, Michael Yussef, John Piper, Chip Ingrim, Steve Brown, Tim Keller, Stephen Arterburn, James and Ryan Dobson, Beth Moore, R.C. Sproul, Alister Begg, Max Lacado, Timothy Keller, Philip Yancey, Bill and Glorida Gaither—my supervising teachers when I student-taught—through the years innumerable blessings from their music: sound bites from your music echo in my heart and have found their way into these pages, Bradlee Hedrick for your inspirational piano music.

A song recorded by the Gaithers—"Sitting at the Feet of Jesus"—has captured my heart and imagination.

Those who relentlessly proclaim Truth transport me again and again into His presence.

Thank you, all of you.

You may contact the author at the following e-mail address:

linda.inhispresence.warner@gmail.com

About the Author

Linda Warner grew up on a small sheep farm in northern Wisconsin. From earliest childhood, she longed to teach, often "tormenting" her nieces and nephew in her eagerness to play school—they were her willing, and admittedly yes, sometimes unwilling students, and she was the one in charge of the classroom.

Because she loved the written word, she chose high school English. Adapting her teaching style after that of Bill and Gloria Gaither—her supervising teachers while at Taylor University—she began a long career of encouraging others to write. In 2002, she received a Coca Cola Teacher of the Year Award while at Westminster Christian School in Miami, Florida. But her greatest reward is the memory of precious relationships with hundreds of students, and along with them, acknowledging God as the Word, the Great Communicator.

As the wonder of Christ's grace filled her imagination, she had no choice but to express this passion for Him; thus, these stories emerged as devotionals.

During a difficult time in the life of a loved close relative, she sent him some of the stories. His response astounded and thrilled her. "I've accepted Christ as Savior," he called to say one morning, "and your stories brought me to this place."

When her son Timothy urged publication, she answered: "God used these words once in a way that brought eternal impact. If He would be pleased to use them again, I could only give Him glory. It's all about Him."

Linda lives with husband Paul in Lake Mary, Florida. She still teaches English part-time at Orangewood Christian School. She enjoys spending time with her son Dan and his wife Joan and taking trips to Atlanta to visit Timothy, his wife Joy, and two grandsons Aiden and Peyton.

LaVergne, TN USA
26 May 2010
184071LV00003B/2/P